Projects for Pr[...]
Blackline Master Spa[...]
for Middle Schoo[...]

PASO A PASO

A/B

Harriet Schottland Barnett
Manhattanville College
Purchase, NY
formerly of the Dobbs Ferry (NY) Public Schools

Christine S. Wells
Cheyenne Mountain Junior High School
Colorado Springs, CO

ScottForesman
A Division of HarperCollinsPublishers

Editorial Offices: Glenview, Illinois

Regional Offices: San Jose, California • Atlanta, Georgia
Glenview, Illinois • Oakland, New Jersey • Dallas, Texas

Visit ScottForesman's Home Page at http://www.scottforesman.com

ISBN: 0-673-20798-6

Front Cover Photo: (l) © Sherlyn Bjorkgren/DDB Stock Photo; (r) © Ken Laffal

1.800.554.4411
http://www.scottforesman.com

12345678910-MH-05040302010099989796

Table of Contents

Projects for Proficiency

Introduction

To make the best use of these projects for proficiency, begin by going through the Table of Contents to familiarize yourself with the blackline masters available. Leaf through the projects themselves in order to decide when to use them. The textbook inventory (page 1) and the name plate (page 4), for example, are suitable for the very first days of class.

Check the Objective and Applications sections for additional ideas for when and how to use the projects. For example, the Applications sections of the game board (page 24), the number cube (page 26), and the grids for graphs/puzzles/word games (page 42) all suggest ways to introduce, review, and recycle material in enjoyable, easy-to-manage game situations. These sections will also help you decide which activities would best complement each chapter or theme and which would be most useful for each of your classes.

There are cross references to this book in the teacher's editions of *Paso a paso A* and *B* and of the *Writing, Audio & Video Activities Workbook* that accompanies the program. There you will find suggestions for which project to use in conjunction with a particular exercise. You may want to mark these sections for future reference.

You may also want to create file folders with multiple copies of projects that you will use often or that have many different uses. For example, you can use the Bingo grid (page 46), the Venn diagram (page 48), and the poll/survey form (page 56) in a wide variety of activities. Preparing such folders is an especially good idea if your school requires advance notice for copies from the duplicating center.

Here is a listing of projects according to the types of activities they are especially suitable for. As you use this book, you will probably want to add other projects to these categories, move projects from one category to another, and perhaps even create additional categories.

Beginning the year
Textbook Inventory
Name Plate
Calendars

Role-plays / dialogues / presentations
Calendars
Clocks
Coat of Arms
Family Tree
Photo Album
Menu
Restaurant Check/Shopping List
TV Program Guide
Poll/Survey Form
Coins and Bills
Speech Balloons
Cartoon Characters

v

Team / group games and activities
Game Board
Number Cube
Recipe Cards
Grids for Graphs/Puzzles/Word Games
Bingo Grid
Venn Diagram
Word Web
Logic Puzzle Matrices
Maps
International Road Signs
Flags
Pronoun Art
Grids for Interdisciplinary Activities

Crafts
Moorish Tiles
Ojos de Dios
Molas
Hand Puppet
Skeleton Puppet
Paper Cutouts and Flowers
Luminarias

Writing activities
Post Card
Greeting Card
Stationery
Invitation
Menu
Restaurant Check/Shopping List
TV Program Guide
Venn Diagram
Word Web
Concrete Poetry
Speech Balloons

For the teacher
Certificate of Merit
Awards
Grids for Interdisciplinary Activities

Textbook Inventory

Objective
To provide an opportunity for students to familiarize themselves with their textbook.

Procedure
Duplicate the Textbook Inventory and hand out copies when you distribute the textbooks. Have students answer questions 1 through 4 in class and answer the remainder for homework (along with putting a cover on the book, if that is required).

After filling out and reviewing the Textbook Inventory, students will feel more comfortable with their books because they will know where and how to find the information they need. They will use their textbooks more often and more efficiently to do assignments both in and outside of class.

Applications
- Discuss the finished inventories in class. Make sure students have their textbook on their desk. Have students tell what they wrote and explain why.

- For several questions answers will vary. Have all students turn to the pages mentioned by different students. This sharing of information will help them become more familiar with the text.

Textbook Inventory

1. What is the title of your textbook? _____

2. What is the last name of at least one author? _____

3. What is the name of the publisher? _____

4. What are three colors that are used on the cover? _____

   _____

5. On what page does the Table of Contents *(Tabla de materias)* begin? _____

6. Look at the *Tabla de materias* and answer the next two questions.

   • How many chapters *(capítulos)* does the book have? _____

   • What is the name of the main section <u>before</u> *Capítulo 1?* _____

   _____

7. Find a page with a map. What is the page number? What does the map show?

   _____

8. Pick any chapter. What number is it? What is the theme? Why do you think so?

   _____

   _____

   _____

9. What are two Objectives for the chapter you have chosen? _____

   _____

   _____

   _____

10. Find a page with a photograph of people or things from a Spanish-speaking country. What is the page number? Give a very brief description of the picture.

_____

_____

_____

The back part of your textbook has several helpful sections.

11. On what page would you start to look for the English equivalent of a Spanish word? What is this section called? Write an example from that section.

_____

_____

_____

12. On what page would you start to look for the Spanish equivalent of an English word? What is this section called? Write an example from that section.

_____

_____

_____

13. On what page would you start to look for help with verbs *(verbos)*? What is this section called?

_____

_____

_____

14. You want to review the days of the week but can't remember the page number. What is the name of the section where you could find this information? On what page does it start?

_____

_____

_____

Congratulations! You know your textbook really well. This will definitely help you learn Spanish more easily.

Name Plate

Objective
To provide visual opportunities to learn classmates' names using name plates.

Procedure
Duplicate and distribute the name plate sheets. Have students hold the sheets horizontally, cut out the name plate along the heavy lines, and fold them on the dotted lines. Students write their English or Spanish name, whichever will be used in class, inside the border. Have them color the border design. Use a small piece of tape to attach the bottom and rear panels, or have students paste plates to cardboard or posterboard for added stability. Students display their completed name plates on their desks.

Applications
- Name plates can be used to help you and the class learn students' names (especially if they are using Spanish names), to identify students for visitors to the classroom, to help parents find their child's desk at Open House, and to simplify things for substitute teachers.

- As students enter the room, distribute the completed name plates at random. Have each student find the person whose name is on the front (*¿Cómo te llamas? Me llamo . . .* or *¿Te llamas . . . ? Sí./No. Me llamo . . .*). If there are assigned seats, once names are more familiar students can simply place the name plates on the correct desks. This activity helps students get to know one another and learn their Spanish names more quickly.

Calendars

Objective
To provide meaningful opportunities to speak and write Spanish using daily, weekly, monthly, and yearly calendars and a weekly homework calendar.

Procedure
Choose the appropriate calendar page, duplicate, and distribute.

Applications

- Students fill out a real or hypothetical **daily** schedule to use as a prop in dialogues.

- Have students fill out the **daily** calendar page according to their school schedule, then pair students to compare classes, times, teachers, homework, etc. Students can also create ideal schedules specially suited to their interests.

- Students can create a personal or school-related diary on the **weekly** calendar.

- Students can keep a **weekly** weather calendar, noting temperatures and weather conditions and illustrating them.

- After filling out **weekly** calendars, pairs or small groups can compare schedules to try to find a mutually convenient time for a shared activity.

- On **monthly** calendar pages, students can record classmates' birthdays, holidays, vacations, school activities, and test dates. Distribute the calendar on the first of each month. Encourage students to put calendars in their notebooks or post them in their lockers to keep Spanish in front of them as much as possible.

- Students work in pairs, using **any calendar** you choose. After each student fills out a calendar, pairs ask each other questions such as *¿Adónde vas el lunes? ¿Qué haces el lunes? ¿Estás ocupado(a) a las cinco? ¿Hay una fiesta en septiembre?* (Questions will depend on the calendar used.) Students can write their partner's responses on a blank calendar and then compare it with the completed calendar.

- To create a **yearly** calendar, have students fill in 12 **monthly** calendar sheets with important events in your school or class or in Spanish-speaking countries.

Día _____

_____

_____

7:00	
7:30	
8:00	
8:30	
9:00	
9:30	
10:00	
10:30	
11:00	
11:30	
12:00	
12:30	
1:00	
1:30	
2:00	
2:30	
3:00	
3:30	
4:00	
4:30	
5:00	
5:30	
6:00	
6:30	
7:00	
7:30	
8:00	
8:30	
9:00	

Esta semana

lunes

martes

miércoles

jueves

viernes

sábado

domingo

Mes:

lunes	martes	miércoles	jueves	viernes	sábado	domingo

Fecha	Día	Clases	Tarea

Días festivos en el mundo hispano

ENERO
1 Año Nuevo
   Día de la Independencia (Cuba)
6 Fiesta de los Reyes Magos
   (Todos los países hispanos)
28 Día de José Martí (Cuba)

FEBRERO
5 Día del Aniversario de la Constitución
   (México)
24 Día de la Bandera (México)
27 Día de la Independencia
   (República Dominicana)

MARZO
1 Día de los Héroes (Paraguay)
19 Día de San José (Todos los países
   hispanos)
21 Día del Aniversario de Benito Juárez
   (México)

ABRIL
1 Día de las Américas (Todos los países
   hispanos)
19 Día de la Firma de la Independencia
   (Venezuela)

MAYO
1 Día del Trabajo (La mayoría de
   los países hispanos)
5 Día de la Victoria de Puebla (México)
14 Día de la Independencia (Paraguay)
21 Día de las Glorias Navales (Chile)
25 Fiesta Patria (Argentina)

JUNIO
12 Día de la Paz (Paraguay)
20 Día de la Bandera (Argentina)
21 Día de San Juan Bautista (patrón de
   Puerto Rico)
29 Día de San Pedro y San Pablo
   (Todos los países hispanos)

JULIO
5 Día de la Independencia (Venezuela)
9 Día de la Independencia (Argentina)
14 Día de la Dignidad Nacional (Nicaragua)
16 Fiesta Patria (Bolivia)
20 Día de la Independencia (Colombia)

24 Día del Aniversario de Simón Bolívar
   (Ecuador y Venezuela)
25 Día del Apóstol Santiago (patrón de
   España y Chile)
28 Día de la Independencia (Perú)

AGOSTO
6 Día de la Independencia (Bolivia)
   Fiestas Patronales (El Salvador)
10 Día de la Independencia (Ecuador)
15 Día de la Asunción de la Virgen
   (La mayoría de los países hispanos)
25 Día de la Independencia (Uruguay)
   Día de la Constitución (Paraguay)
30 Día de Santa Rosa de Lima
   (patrona de Perú)

SEPTIEMBRE
15 Día de la Independencia (Costa Rica,
   El Salvador, Guatemala, Honduras y
   Nicaragua)
16 Día de la Independencia (México)
18 Día de la Independencia (Chile)

OCTUBRE
9 Día de la Dignidad Nacional (Perú)
11 Día de la Revolución (Panamá)
12 Día Nacional (España)
   Día de la Hispanidad (Todos los países
   hispanos)

NOVIEMBRE
1 Día de Todos los Santos
2 Día de los Muertos
3 Día de la Independencia (Panamá)
5 Primer Grito de Independencia
   (El Salvador)

DICIEMBRE
6 Día de la Constitución (España)
8 Día de la Inmaculada Concepción
   (Todos los países hispanos)
12 Día de Nuestra Señora de Guadalupe
   (patrona de México)
16 Primer Día de las Posadas (México)
24 Nochebuena
25 Navidad
31 Víspera de Año Nuevo

Clocks

Objective

To provide meaningful opportunities to speak and write Spanish while learning, reviewing, and reinforcing telling time.

Procedure

Duplicate and distribute clocks. You may want to separate and enlarge them. Students can paste enlarged clocks on paper plates, large index cards, or cardboard, attaching movable hands to the analog clock with brads.

Applications

- Have students work in pairs to alternate giving a time and indicating it on one of the clocks. Then have both students write out in words the times indicated on both clocks. Extend this activity by having students say something they do at that time. Remind them of the difference between "it is" (*es la/son las*) and "at" *(a la/a las)* "o'clock."

- Ask a question such as *¿Cuándo comes el desayuno?* Students indicate their answer on the clock sheet. They can also write the answer in words below the clock. Pairs or groups can compare times indicated to see which appears on most sheets.

- Make a statement about doing something at a certain time. Students working alone, in pairs, or in groups indicate that time on the clock. This is a good listening activity.

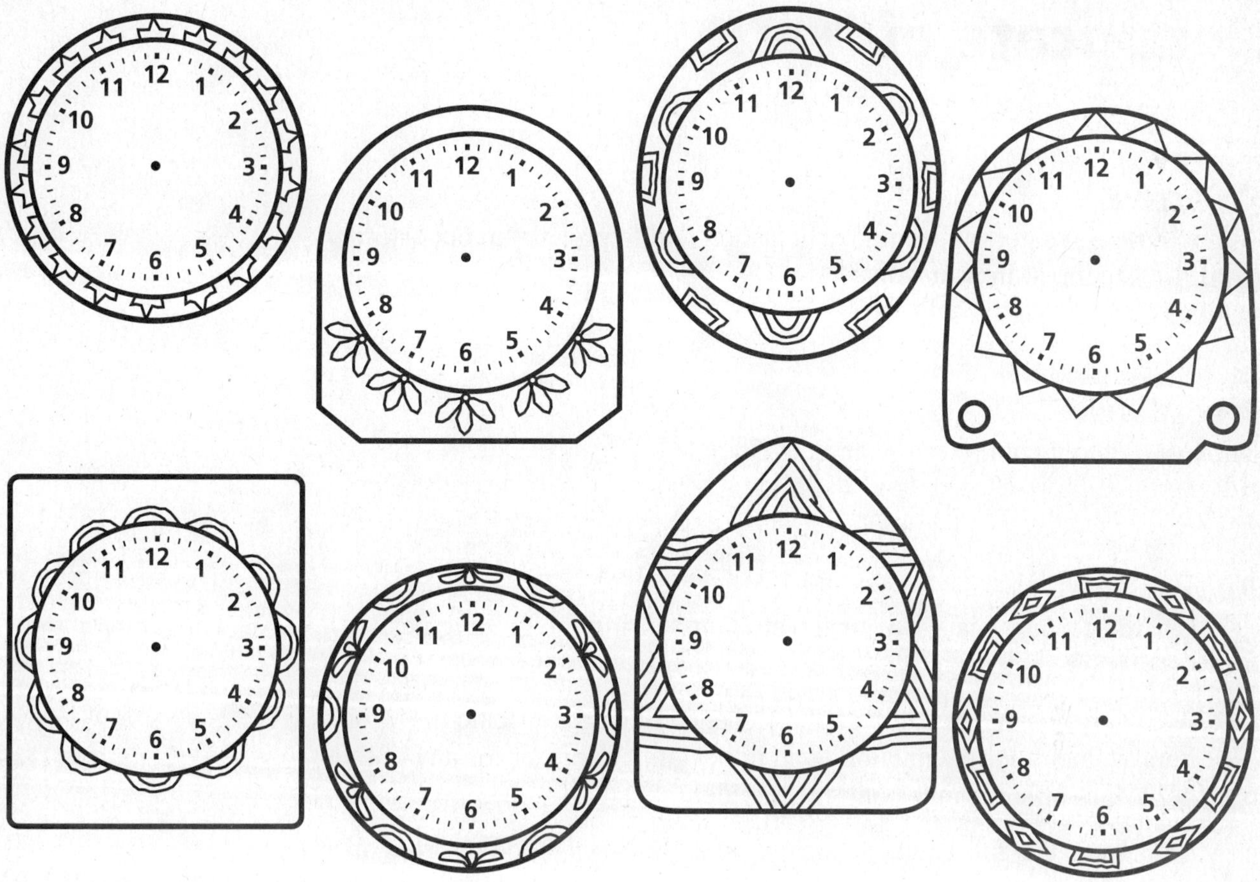

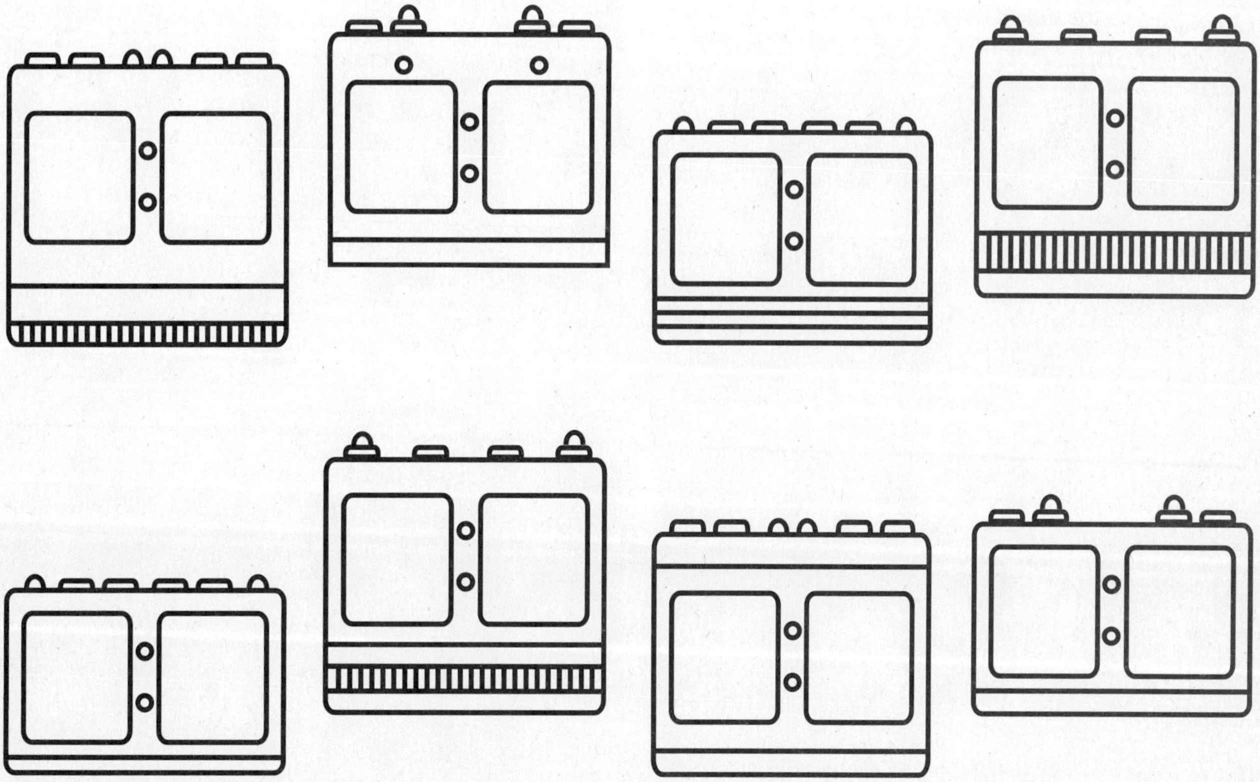

Certificate of Merit

Objective

To encourage greater effort and participation and to provide an opportunity to read a document in Spanish.

Procedure

Duplicate, fill out appropriately, and distribute.

Applications

- Award this certificate to your top students during the grading period, quarter, or semester.

- Award the certificate for overall excellence during a specific time, for improvement, for completion of an important project, or for any of the behaviors or small milestones in a student's year.

- To personalize the merit certificate, color the border, add stickers or gummed stars, or use rubber stamps.

Certificado de Mérito

En honor de su excelente trabajo se presenta a:

el día

del mes de

del año

Firma

Awards

Objective
To acknowledge special effort or performance.

Procedure
Duplicate the awards on page 17. Choose various expressions of approval from the list below and write them on the awards. Or cut 1 1/2"–2" blue ribbon into 3"–4" lengths. Use a permanent marker to write an expression directly on the ribbon. Attach a small safety pin. Prepare these awards in advance and distribute them often.

Applications
- Here are just a few possible reasons for special recognition: good pronunciation, good partnering, excellent participation, helpful tutoring, perfect homework record for a given period, outstanding improvement, outstanding dialogue work, excellent expression, courageous volunteer, extra effort to speak Spanish.

- Attach the awards to homework, quizzes, tests, etc. Present them in class with applause from everyone. Reward those students who do not get on the honor roll but who try hard.

- Use these awards often and reward all students.

Among the possible expressions of approval are:

bien hecho	excepcional	número uno
bravo	fabuloso	perfecto
dinamita	fantástico	primerísimo
encima del mundo	grandísimo éxito	sensacional
especial	increíble	soy el/la mejor
estupendo	lo máximo	super
excelente	magnífico	superbien

Coat of Arms

Objective
To provide opportunities to speak, write, and categorize in Spanish.

Procedure
Duplicate and distribute crests.

Applications
- Have the class decide what the crest should represent. Crests can be used to identify a student as part of a family, class, grade, or team. They can also be used to identify the class as a whole. Some suggestions for visualizable categories include family name, personal goals, autobiographical events, favorite activities, holidays, foods, kinds of music, school subjects, school name, popular sports, and seasons. A Spanish class crest might include a map of South America, a flag, a favorite Mexican food, and so on. Here are some examples of ways to divide a shield.

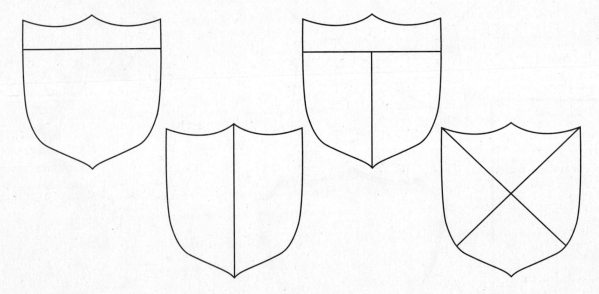

- Display crests in the classroom, halls, or school offices.

- Have students explain their crests to partners or small groups. For example, *En mi escudo hay un libro porque me gusta leer...*

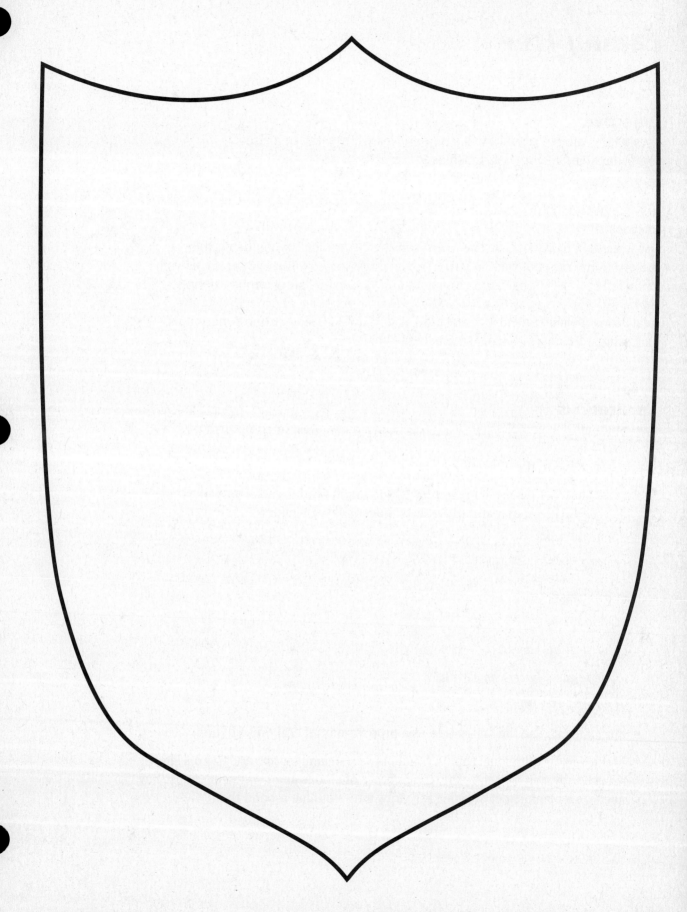

Family Tree

Objective
To practice family vocabulary and possessives while creating a visual representation of family relationships.

Procedure
Duplicate and distribute. Be especially sensitive to students when doing this activity. Some may not want to share personal information. Encourage the use of an imaginary or fictional family. You may want to provide a humorous example: *Gloria Estefan es mi mamá y Antonio Banderas es mi papá.* Decide how many relatives you want students to include, but be sure they show three generations, including at least grandparents, parents, and children.

Applications
- Students can complete the tree with drawings, photos, or cutout pictures in each blank. They can label each relative with the person's name and age or relationship to the student or other focal person.

- Have students choose one member of the family whom they would like to describe. They may want to use these questions as a guide:

    ¿Cómo se llama?

    ¿Cuál es la fecha de su cumpleaños?

    ¿Dónde vive?

    ¿Cómo es?

    ¿Qué le gusta hacer?

    ¿Qué te gusta hacer con él (ella)?

    ¿Qué deportes le gustan?

- Students can use the family tree as a prop for a brief oral presentation.

- Make several additional copies. Students whose families are not appropriately reflected by this tree can paste the number of circles and connecting lines they need on a blank sheet of paper and draw a tree outline around them.

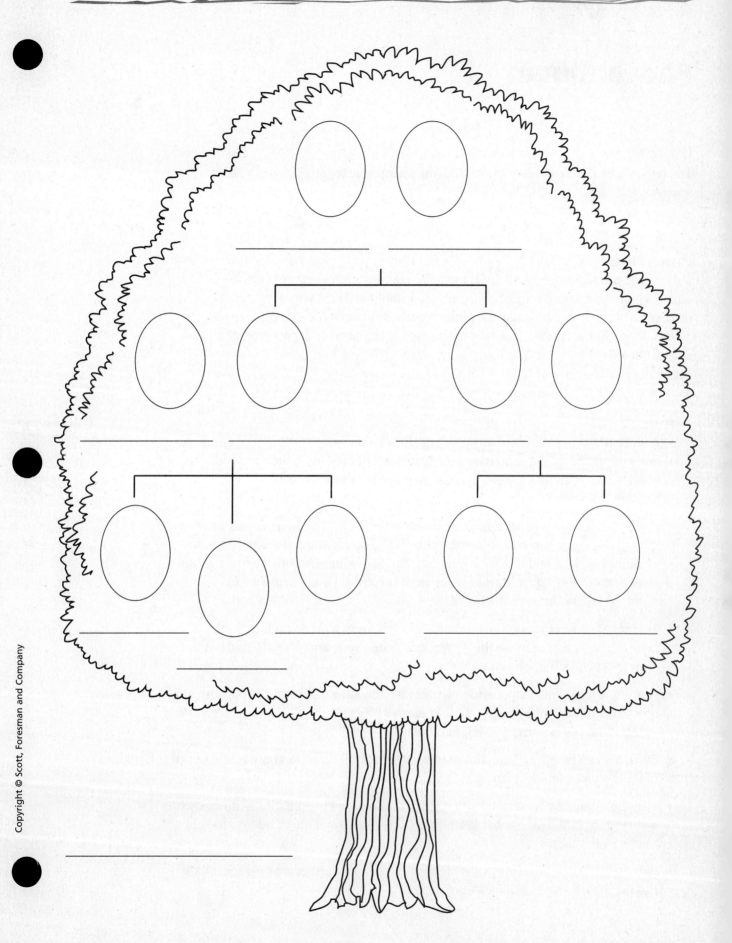

Photo Album

Objective

To speak and write Spanish while organizing visually, categorizing, or creating a story.

Procedure

Decide what activity the photo album will be used for and whether it will be an individual or a group project. Once this is established and you have given instructions and any additional vocabulary, distribute copies of the photo album page. You may want to increase the size of the page to accommodate larger photos.

Applications

- A student or group of students can draw or use magazine pictures of families, animals, vacation spots, activities, or items in any category, such as food, clothing, or rooms in a house. They can label the pictures or give them to another student or group to label.

- A student or group of students can attach pictures to the photo album page to create a story. For example, the story based on pictures of a boy swimming, skiing, in school, and in a park might be the following: *Esteban nada en el mar en el verano. Esquía en las montañas en el invierno. Va al parque en la primavera. Va a la escuela en el otoño.*

- You can give the page to the students and tell them what to include in the album. They can complete the artwork as homework and prepare to describe it orally in class the following day.

- A group of students can provide pictures for the album. Another group can ask questions based on the page: *¿Qué es esto?, ¿Te gusta . . . ?, ¿Cuál . . . te gusta más?, ¿Cuándo lo llevas (comes, haces)?*

- Students can use the photo album instead of a family tree to show actual photos of their own or an ideal family.

- Use the album for pictures or photographs of famous people. Students can write a short biography on the back. Or give students several short biographies to match to the pictures.

- As a writing task students can write more extensive captions or paragraphs for the pictures on a separate sheet of paper.

Game Board

Objective
To provide opportunities to speak, read, and listen to Spanish while interacting in a game situation.

Procedure
Duplicate the game board outline to create a complete game with a starting and an ending box. Draw lines to create game board boxes. Indicate the tasks students will perform. (See the list of suggested tasks below.) Duplicate and distribute the board along with the Number Cube on page 27.

Applications
- Have students play in groups of four, each student using an identifiable coin or other marker. Students take turns throwing the number cube and moving their markers the number of spaces indicated on the cube. They must read and perform the task indicated in the box they land on. If a student does not perform the task, he or she loses a turn. The student who reaches the end of the board first is the winner. The winners of each group can play for the class championship. Tasks might be to change an infinitive to a specific tense and person, give a complete sentence using the indicated word, name the weather or season for an article of clothing indicated, name the country for the capital or flag indicated. The possibilities are endless, depending only on the materials to be practiced or reviewed.

- Distribute blank game boards so that pairs or groups can write in the tasks and then invite another pair or group to play the game.

Possible tasks

Appropriate response to ¡Hola! ¿Qué tal?

¿Qué día es . . . ?

¿Cuál es la fecha de hoy?

¿Ocho + veintiséis = . . . ?

¿5+17 = ?

¿Cómo se escribe . . . ?

¿Cuáles son los números de 1 a 30?

¿Cuántos días hay en . . . ?

Recita el alfabeto.

¿Te gusta . . . ?

¿Qué te gusta más, . . . o . . . ?

¿Qué te gusta hacer?

Possible labels

Regresa a . . .

2 (3, 4) para atrás

2 (3, 4) para adelante

Pierdes un turno.

¡Luz roja! ¡Para!

¡Luz verde! Sigue.

Empieza aquí.

¡Fin!

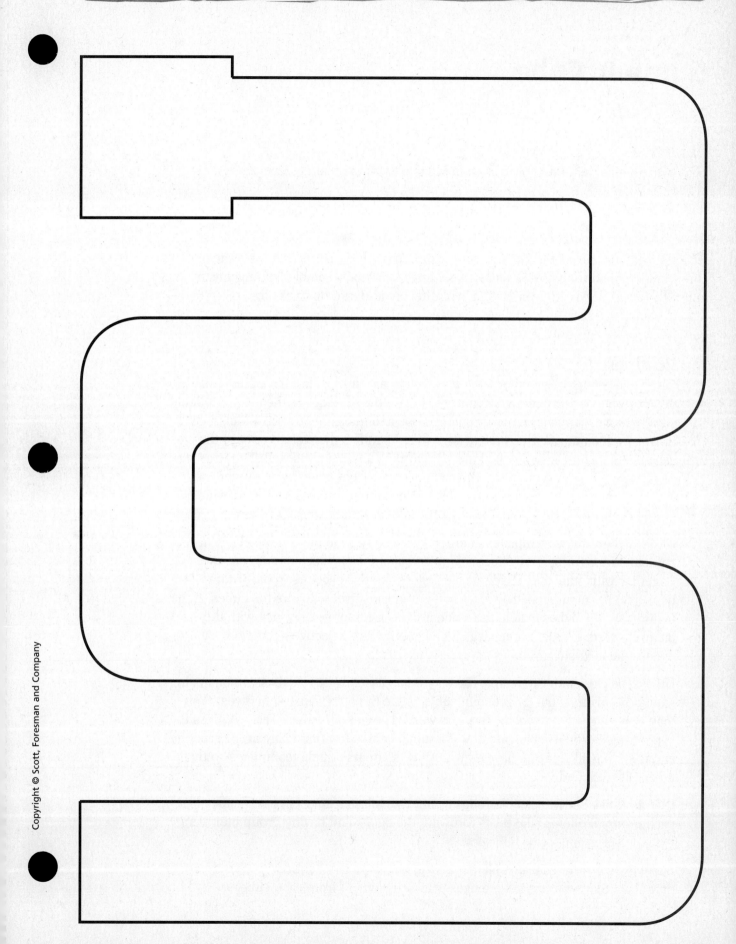

Number Cube

Objective
To practice vocabulary and verb forms and to use them to create sentences.

Procedure
Duplicate and distribute the number cube template. Help students assemble their cubes by demonstrating how to cut, fold, and paste or tape a sample. You may want to use the cube alone or in conjunction with the Game Board on page 25.

Applications
- Give each group one number cube template to assemble. First have students draw or write six different vocabulary items on the six sides of the cube. Students choose one group member to throw the cube and guess in Spanish which picture or word will come up. The student who wins identifies the picture or says the word. You may want students to use the word in a sentence as well. The winning student gets a point and throws the cube next. Play continues, with students guessing before each throw which side will come up. In case of multiple winners, students each receive a point and take turns throwing the cube.

- Give each group two templates in order to create two identical cubes. First have students draw the same six vocabulary items on the six sides of both cubes. Together with students, decide on a category (clothing, colors, rooms of the house, family members). To play, a student in each group throws the cubes. If the pictures on the cubes match, the student gives a complete sentence with the pictured word. (Students can also add an appropriate adjective.) If they don't match, the next student takes a turn.

- Divide the class into two teams. Have students assemble two cubes. On one cube should be written noun or pronoun subjects; on the other cube, infinitives. (You may want to specify a specific tense as well.) Throw both cubes. Team A gives the appropriate verb form indicated by the subject cube. Continue playing, alternating teams so that all students have a turn. Allow students to help teammates so that no one is excluded.

- Play as above but with small groups rather than class teams. Give two cubes to each group. Students take turns throwing the cubes and having group members give the verbs and forms indicated.

- Small groups or class teams play as above, but add a third cube with object pronouns. Students create sentences using an element from each cube.

TAB

TAB

TAB

Post Card

Objective
To provide opportunities to write brief correspondence in Spanish.

Procedure
Duplicate and distribute copies of the post card template. Help students cut out the card along the heavy lines and then fold it along the dotted line. Space for the message and address will be on one side and space for the picture on the other. Students paste or tape the folded post card together. They may want to paste a piece of thin cardboard between the two sides for added stability.

Here is some useful post card vocabulary students may want:

Greetings
¡Hola . . . !
Querido(a) / (os) / (as) . . . :

Possible messages
Aquí estoy en . . .
Lo estoy pasando muy bien.
Hace . . . / Llueve / Nieva.

Closings
Saludos
Cariños
Recuerdos
Un beso
Un abrazo

Applications
- Students pick a Spanish-speaking city, resort, or other place of interest and illustrate it on the blank side. On the other side they write a message and address. They may want to design a stamp as well.

- Students write a card to an out-of-town friend, describing an interesting upcoming or past event.

- "Send" completed post cards to classmates or to students in another Spanish class, who should respond with cards of their own.

- Write the names of various places on slips of paper. Each group picks one and draws an appropriate illustration. You might use locales familiar to students or others that they might need to research. Students write a message and address and deliver their card to another group.

- More advanced students might include a very brief description at the top of the message side such as one might find on a printed post card.

MENSAJE

SELLO

DIRECCIÓN

Greeting Card

Objective

To write greetings in Spanish for various holidays and special occasions.

Procedure

Enlarge, duplicate, and distribute the greeting card template. Have students cut out the pattern along the heavy lines and then fold it along the dotted lines so that a border appears on the front.

Here are some words and expressions that students might need:

Querido /(a) /(os) /(as) . . .　　*Feliz Día de la Madre (del Padre, del Abuelo)*
Feliz Cumpleaños　　　　　　　*celebrar*
Feliz Navidad　　　　　　　　　*con cariño*
Feliz (Próspero) Año Nuevo　　*¡Felicitaciones!*
Feliz Día de San Valentín

Applications

- With students, decide on the occasion and some possible illustrations and messages.

- Have students make cards in class and/or at home. You may want to put names in a hat and have students select the recipient of the card. Make extra holiday cards for administrators, faculty, and other school personnel.

- Have students make holiday cards for students in a bilingual primary class and deliver them in person.

- Have the class make holiday cards for Spanish-speaking hospital or nursing home patients or for people at a senior center.

Stationery

Objective

To provide opportunities to correspond in Spanish.

Procedure

Duplicate and distribute the letter format to each student. Encourage them to personalize their letters. Offer markers, stickers, glitter, or rubber stamps.

Here are some words and expressions students may need for their letters:

¡Hola . . . !   *Recuerdos*
Querido /(a) / (os) / (as) . . . :   *Un beso*
Saludos   *Un abrazo*
Cariños

Applications

- Set up a classroom post office, mailbox, or note board to encourage written correspondence in Spanish within the class or between classes. Be sure that you write notes too to make sure that no one is left out.

- Have students write letters to exchange with Spanish students in another school.

- Have students write to students at a school in another state. Contact teachers at conferences or through The American Association of Teachers of Spanish and Portuguese (Gunter Hall 106; University of Northern Colorado; Greeley, CO 80639). You may also want to send a videotape of a tour of your school. If so, make sure that all of your students introduce themselves and give some additional information *(¡Hola! Me llamo . . . Soy . . .)*.

- Explore the possibility of establishing pen pals in Spanish-speaking countries. Contact the school program of the Peace Corps (U.S. Peace Corps—World Wise Schools; Attn: Scott Lozen; 1990 K Street NW; Washington, D.C. 20256; E-mail:slozen@peacecorps.gov). The program will connect your school with a volunteer in the country of your choice. Your class then corresponds directly with the volunteer.

- Have students create a design or picture for a stamp to decorate their letters or envelopes. The theme could be a current or historical figure, landmark, special event, or place.

_____ *de* _____ *de 19* _____

_____ :

_____

_____

_____

_____

_____

_____

_____

_____

_____

_____ ,

_____

Invitation

Objective

To use written Spanish in an invitation to a special event.

Procedure

Duplicate and distribute the invitation template. Have students cut out the pattern along the heavy lines and then fold it along the dotted lines, so that the border appears on the front and the writing lines appear on the inside.

Here is a list of words and expressions students may need:

Invitación	*¡Fiesta!*
Para ti	*¡Fiesta de (cumpleaños, sorpresa, fin de año,*
¿Vienes?	*graduación, disfraces)!*
¡Celebremos!	*Picnic*

Students may want to handwrite one of the following at the bottom of the invitation:

Por favor, llama al _____ para confirmar.

¡Cada uno trae algo! ¿Puedes traer _____ ?

Here is a sample invitation filled out:

En ocasión de:

_____ *mi cumpleaños* _____

Día: _____ *sábado, 23 de octubre* _____

_____

Hora: _____ *8:00* _____

Lugar: _____ *247 Spring Street* _____

_____

Por favor, llama al 555-1913 para confirmar.

Applications

- Individuals or groups can create invitations for a party (class, holiday, birthday, graduation, surprise, Halloween) and deliver them to another Spanish class or to faculty members.

- The class could volunteer to make invitations for a special school event or celebration.

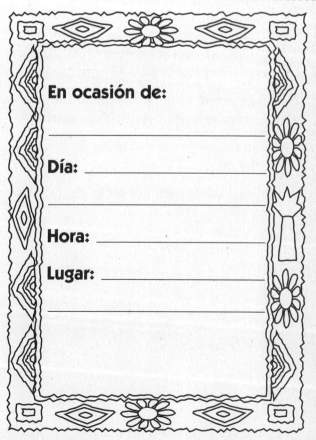

En ocasión de:

_____

Día: _____

_____

Hora: _____

Lugar: _____

_____

Recipe Cards

Objective
To provide opportunities for cooking in or out of class using recipes for four simple dishes.

Before you begin a cooking project with your students, be sure to investigate and fulfill all the requirements of your school with regard to cooking, electrical appliances, and so on.

Procedure
Cooking with students can be fun, rewarding, and educational if proper preparation is done ahead of time. It is easiest in a kitchen, where facilities for food storage and cleanup are available. However, cooking, serving, and cleanup are all possible in a regular classroom setting if a hot plate and other small appliances are permissible. The recipes included here have been field-tested and will be successful in a classroom. *¡Buen provecho!*

Applications
- Use these recipes to prepare food for a class or school party, holiday celebration, or other special event. You may want to add a *licuado* (see page 173 of *Paso a paso A)* or make a prepackaged *flan*.

- Invite parent volunteers to help. They can monitor the hot stove, supervise cleanup, or give a cooking demonstration.

- Send recipes home and invite families to send a note verifying the success of the dish.

- Provide the opportunity for students to find other recipes via the computer or in the library.

Salsa

3 cups canned tomatoes
1 teaspoon salt
1 teaspoon garlic powder
1/2 teaspoon oregano

1/2 teaspoon cumin
1/4 cup chopped onion
2–3 chopped jalapeño peppers

Place all ingredients in the blender and mix. Serve with tortillas or tortilla chips. Makes 3 cups.

Gazpacho

1 cup tomato juice
3/4 cup chopped cucumber
1 tablespoon wine vinegar

1/2 teaspoon salt
1/4 teaspoon pepper
1 small chopped tomato

Place all ingredients in the blender and mix. Makes 1 1/2 cups.

Guacamole

3 ripe avocados
1 ripe tomato
2 green onions

5 green chilies
1 teaspoon salt
1 teaspoon lemon juice

Peel avocados, dice tomato, chop green onions fine. Add chopped green chilies, salt, and lemon juice. Add all ingredients to avocados and mash together. Serve with tortillas or tortilla chips.

Rice and Beans

3 tablespoons oil
2 cloves garlic, crushed
1 large green pepper, chopped
2 cans black beans

1/2 teaspoon oregano
3 tablespoons vinegar
3 cups hot cooked rice

Heat oil in saucepan and sauté garlic and green pepper until softened. Add the beans, oregano, and vinegar, and simmer until heated through. Serve over rice. Makes 6 servings.

Menu

Objective

To provide opportunities to speak and write in Spanish using a blank menu.

Procedure

Duplicate and distribute menu templates.

Applications

- Have pairs or groups fill in the menu with appropriate headings, foods, and prices. They might illustrate their menus with pictures of foods or by creating a restaurant logo. The menu can then become a prop in a role-play situation in which one student plays the waiter or waitress and the other plays a customer. Provide plastic or paper dishes, cutlery, cups and/or glasses, and even a tablecloth and napkins to enhance the sense of a real restaurant setting.

- Videotape the role-plays and share them with other classes and with parents at Open House or other school functions.

Restaurant Check / Shopping List

Objective
To provide opportunities to categorize and to practice numbers in Spanish using a blank list form.

Procedure
Duplicate and distribute the form.

Applications
- Have students work in pairs or groups to create a restaurant check. They should write down the dishes ordered and then determine the prices. They might use the restaurant check together with the menu on page 39.

- Use the form as a shopping list for clothing. Have pairs or groups create a list of clothing items and prices. Another pair can pretend to have a certain amount of money with which to buy items from the list.

- Use the form as a grocery list. Have one pair create the list and a second pair decide which meal the first pair is shopping for.

- Use the form to reinforce math skills. Have students calculate tips (at 15% of the total), discounts on prices, or possible sales tax.

- Have students use the completed grocery list, clothing list, or restaurant check as a prop in a role-play.

- Have each student list supplies he or she bought for school. Have pairs compare similarities and differences in their purchases. Students can use the Venn diagram on page 49 for their comparisons.

_____

_____

Grids for Graphs/Puzzles/Word Games

Objective
To provide opportunities for communicating in Spanish through word games, puzzles, graphing, and mapping activities.

Procedure
Choose the **grid** on page 44 or the **word square game board** on page 45. Duplicate and distribute. Make sure students understand the rules for the particular game or activity. You may want to put a grid on the overhead projector so the whole class can create and solve a puzzle or word search.

Applications

Graphing
- Have students use the Poll/Survey Form on page 57 to collect data. Have them graph the results on a grid to share with the group or class.

Floor plans or maps
- Individuals, pairs, or small groups make a floor plan or map on the grid. They may design and label an ideal bedroom or house, show the layout of a store or school, or give locations in a city or town.

- Students present their plans orally to the group or class and respond to questions or comments.

- Have students write a description to accompany their plan. Collect the plans and descriptions and scramble each set. Other students then read the descriptions and pick the matching plan.

- Working in pairs, one student describes his or her completed plan. The other draws a plan based on the description without seeing the original. Students then compare the finished drawing to the original.

- After students draw and label the school layout, have pairs ask and answer questions about getting from one class, room, or office to another. This activity is a good review of *tú* commands and prepositions of location.

Crossword puzzles
- Give each student pair a grid. Pairs choose a number of Spanish vocabulary words or verb forms and write accompanying numbered clues. Students can write verbal clues or use the Art BLMs for visual clues. For more advanced

students, you might require complete Spanish sentences for the clues. Have pairs outline on the paper the squares that will be filled in and write numbers in them to indicate the start of the words. They should color in the squares that will not be part of the words. Collect and redistribute the crossword puzzles so that each pair works a puzzle created by someone else.

- Collect the puzzles, photocopy them, and distribute one each day as a class warmup activity or homework assignment.

- Use the creation and solving of crossword puzzles as review activities before a quiz or test.

Scrambled words

- Give each student pair a grid. Have pairs choose a number of Spanish vocabulary words. After writing each word in scrambled order on the paper, one letter per square, pairs can exchange papers and unscramble the words. Using grids for such activities enables all students, especially those needing extra help, to organize and keep track of the letters.

Word search

- Give each student pair a grid. Have pairs choose 20 Spanish vocabulary words, which they write on the paper, one letter per square. The words can be written vertically, horizontally, diagonally, or backwards. Students fill in the remainder of the squares with randomly chosen letters. Have students list the words used in the word search on the back of the paper. Collect the completed word searches and redistribute them so that each pair has one created by another pair of students. To solve, students find and circle all the words. The first pair to finish is the winner.

- Have students create and solve word search puzzles as a pre-quiz review. Extend the activity by having them use each of the listed words in a sentence.

Creative crossword

- Duplicate the game board on page 45. You may want to think of it as Scrabble® without the letter tiles. First demonstrate the game using an overhead projector as you play against the class. Write a Spanish word on the game board, one letter in each square. Place one letter of the first word in the outlined square in the center of the game board. Total the score for your word, and challenge the class to continue, building on your word. Clarify the rules: Are two-letter words allowed? Can just a single letter be added to form a new word? To distinguish between players, use different color pens. The player with the highest score at the end of a set time period wins.

- Duplicate and distribute copies of the game board to pairs or groups of three or four. You may want to reduce the number of squares by outlining only certain of them. Set a time limit, and remind players to use different color pencils or pens.

10	1	3	1	6	2	1	1	1	5	1	1	4	1	5	3	1	1	10
1	6	7	4	2	1	4	6	7	1	3	2	7	1	2	1	3	4	6
3	1	1	1	2	1	5	3	1	1	2	1	1	6	3	2	7	1	1
1	2	1	2	1	1	2	1	1	7	1	3	4	1	2	1	1	3	1
2	1	6	1	2	1	1	3	2	1	1	2	1	1	1	2	1	1	3
1	3	1	1	1	2	2	1	1	4	1	3	2	1	1	6	1	4	1
4	1	1	1	2	5	1	2	1	1	3	1	5	1	3	1	1	1	1
1	4	1	1	8	1	1	3	1	1	1	2	1	6	1	1	4	1	2
1	1	2	1	1	1	5	2	1	1	1	1	1	1	1	5	1	1	1
1	2	3	2	1	4	1	1	1	**1**	1	1	1	4	1	2	1	1	4
3	1	1	9	1	1	1	1	1	1	1	1	5	1	1	2	1	1	2
2	1	6	1	3	2	1	6	2	1	2	1	3	1	1	3	1	1	3
1	3	1	2	1	9	1	1	6	1	4	2	1	1	2	6	1	4	1
1	1	2	1	1	3	7	1	1	3	2	1	1	2	3	1	1	2	1
1	2	1	3	1	2	1	1	2	1	1	5	1	1	1	1	1	1	1
2	1	1	4	1	5	1	1	4	1	1	1	3	1	1	1	1	6	2
4	1	1	8	1	1	1	3	2	4	1	2	1	7	1	1	5	1	4
1	1	4	1	1	1	1	2	1	1	1	4	1	1	1	1	3	1	1
2	6	1	7	1	3	1	1	1	1	2	1	1	1	3	4	1	1	2
10	1	7	1	6	1	3	1	1	6	1	1	4	1	5	2	1	3	10

Bingo Grid

Objective

To provide opportunities for reinforcing vocabulary and grammar and developing listening skills.

Procedure

Duplicate and distribute a grid to each student. Write 25 items to be reviewed on the chalkboard or on a separate sheet. You may want students to generate the list. Students then choose any 16 items from the list and write them anywhere on their grid.

Use index cards to make a calling card for each of the 25 items. Keep track of the items called so you can check for accuracy when students say them back. Play using Bingo rules. Students put a small check in each box containing a word that you call. To win, a student must check four boxes in a row, horizontally, vertically, or diagonally. If a student indicates that he or she has Bingo but is mistaken, the student is out for the rest of that round. This discourages wild guessing and keeps the class attentive. The winning student should say the words back correctly in Spanish, or you may want to require a correct sentence using the words.

Have students remove the check marks before the next round. To avoid confusion, choose different symbols for each round (an X, a circle, a star, etc.), and have students remove them after the round. You may prefer to have students use tokens or markers to cover the boxes rather than write symbols.

Applications

- The possibilities are almost endless, depending upon what you want to review. Suggestions for the 25 items include vocabulary words, verb forms, numbers, countries, capitals, or important cultural sites.

- You may want students needing extra help to work in pairs rather than individually.

- Students may want to create grids using Art BLMs, their own drawings, or magazine pictures of vocabulary items instead of words. Make sure they make calling cards for all 25 items.

- Use the grid as the basis for a scavenger hunt. In the boxes, write the items to be found, then duplicate and distribute the grids to individuals, pairs, or groups.

Bingo

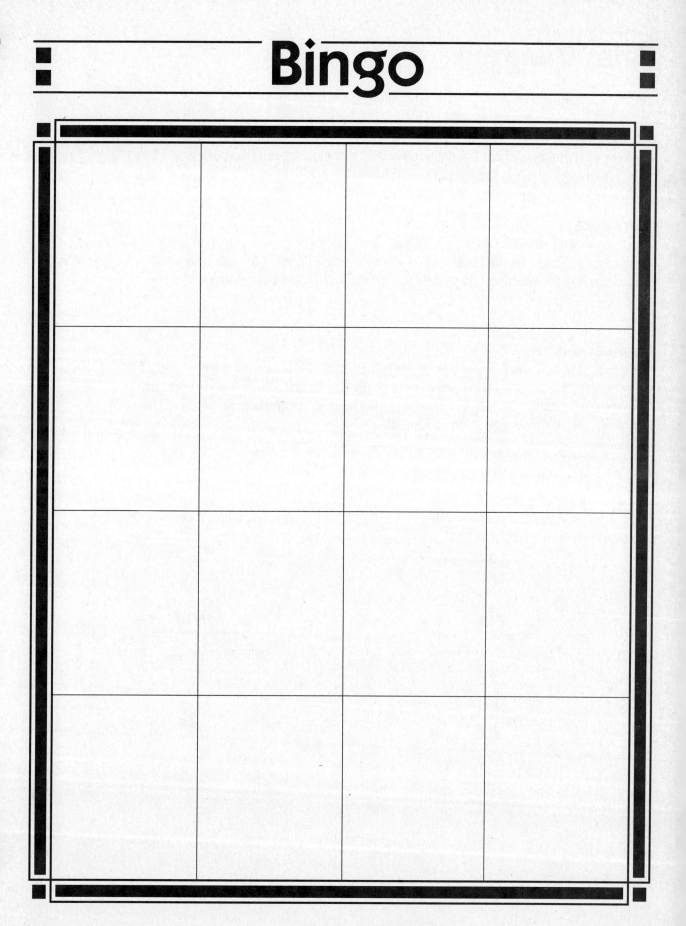

Venn Diagram

Objective
To show differences and commonalities visually by using a Venn diagram.

Procedure
Duplicate and distribute the diagram to pairs or groups. Determine the category, and have students label the circles. Students write the shared characteristics or preferences in the central, overlapping area, and those that differ in the two side areas.

Applications
- Have students work in pairs or teams to compare items needed for two school subjects, favorite weekend activities, favorite foods, schools in the U.S. and in Mexico, natural resources of two countries, and so forth. Have students discuss their conclusions in Spanish or English.

- Put a copy of the diagram on an overhead projector and have the class as a whole do a comparison.

Here is an example of a partially filled-in Venn diagram comparing living room and bedroom furnishings.

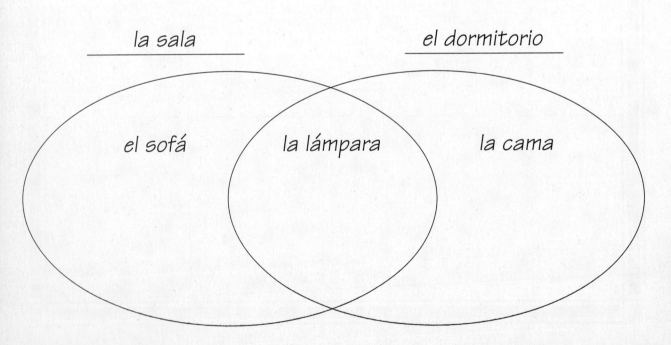

Word Web

Objective
To help students organize their thoughts visually by using a word web.

Procedure
Duplicate and distribute the web. Have students write the main theme or question in the center. In the surrounding circles, they write key words or phrases pertaining to the central theme. You (or students) may add or delete circles as needed for the activity.

Applications
- Have groups choose a central question: *¿Qué piensas hacer este verano?* Group members may respond by writing a verb *(nadar)* or a phrase *(ir a la playa)* in the circles.

- Students can use the web to analyze a story. They write the title in the center and fill in the circles with statements about when and where the story takes place, the main theme, the main character, and so on. Or students can write the name of the main character in the center and complete the circles with how this person feels, acts, looks, and so forth.

- Use the web for organizing interdisciplinary activities. Write the central question or theme in the center and the disciplines involved and the concepts to be dealt with in the circles.

Here is an example of a partially filled-in word web dealing with the home.

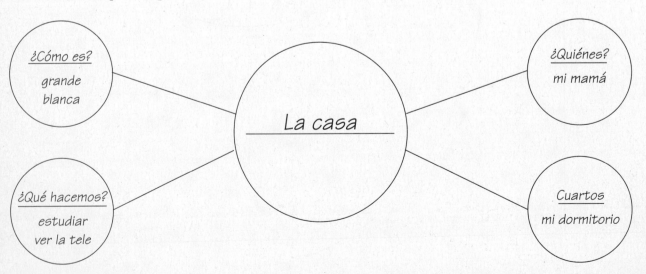

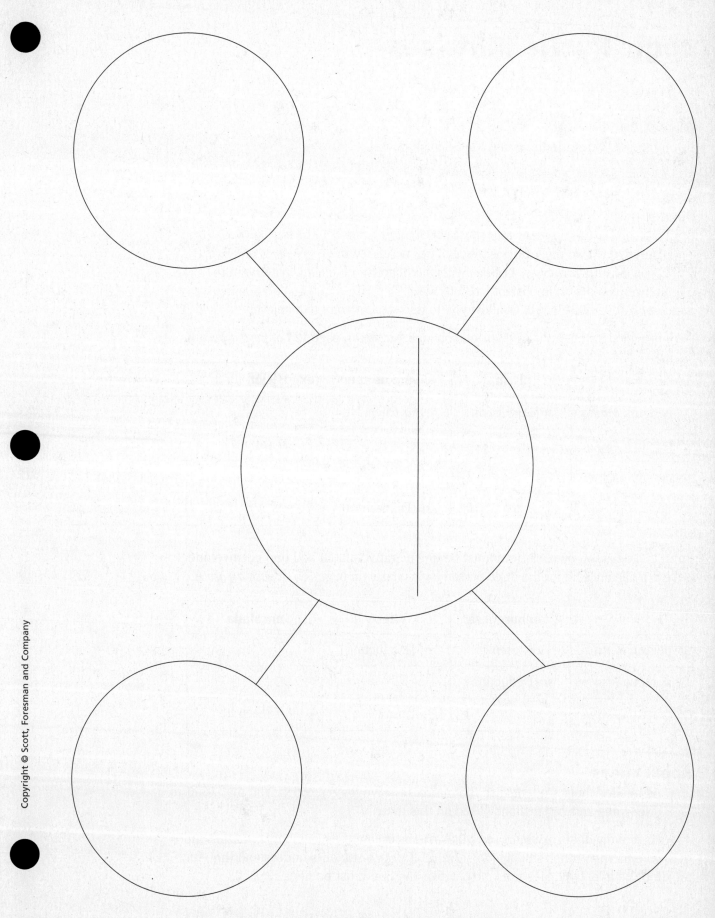

Logic Puzzle Matrices

Objective
To engage in critical thinking tasks in Spanish.

Procedure
Duplicate either the three- or four-person matrix on page 53. For four people, three clues are given. Two must be positive, linking people to their matches, and one must prohibit a match. **Step 1:** Start with the negative clue, and write *no* in the box that represents an impossible match. **Step 2:** Write *sí* for the two positive matches. These three matches allow you to deduce the complete answer.

Here is a filled-in matrix for the four-person logic puzzle on page 124 of *Paso a paso* A.

	piscina	cancha de tenis	exposición de arte	concierto
1ª persona *Marta*	*sí* [Deduction]	*no* [Step 1]		
1ª persona *Pablo*			*sí* [Step 2]	
3ª persona *Pilar*				*sí* [Step 2]
4ª persona *Jorge*		*sí* [Deduction]		

For a three-person puzzle, there must be one negative match and one positive one. Here is a filled-in grid for the three-person logic puzzle on page 165 of *Paso a paso* A.

	hamburguesa	queso	ensalada
1ª persona *Luis*	*no* [Step 1]	*sí* [Deduction]	
2ª persona *Martín*	*sí* [Deduction]		
3ª persona *David*			*sí* [Step 2]

Applications
- As needed, help students use the matrix to solve logic puzzles. You may want to offer hints and suggestions based on this matrix.

- Have individuals, partners, or small groups create their own logic puzzles and give them to other students to solve. Make sure students understand that, for four people, two clues must be positive and one must be negative.

1ª persona			
2ª persona			
3ª persona			

1ª persona				
2ª persona				
3ª persona				
4ª persona				

TV Program Guide

Objective

To use grids to organize information for activities practicing time, duration, and types of programs in Spanish.

Procedure

Duplicate and distribute grids to pairs or groups.

Applications

- Have pairs or groups plan a TV schedule for any four-hour period. The most basic task is for students to choose real or invented programs for the four hours on a single channel on a single day. To increase the complexity, you may want students to choose a day and give listings for several channels, or choose a channel and give listings for several days. To begin filling out the grid, have students write either *Canal* or *Día* in the top left-hand box. Along the top of the form, students list program starting times in half-hour increments.

- Have student groups imagine that they are television producers for a new network. They have to plan programs for their Spanish-speaking audiences from 6 to 10 P.M. They can show movies, sports events, sitcoms, news shows, cartoons, interviews, music videos, or whatever types of programs they choose. Have them fill in the grid with the channel, times, program titles, and perhaps a brief synopsis of each program.

- Assign each of seven groups a different day of the week, and have them plan a TV schedule for that day. Put all the work together in a booklet for parents and other classes to enjoy.

- Use the completed TV schedules as props for skits. Pairs can choose roles (parent and child, two friends, two siblings) and decide which shows to watch.

- Students may prepare posters or video commercials to promote their programs.

- Have students interview each other about their TV-viewing habits. Use questions such as *¿Cuántas horas por día/semana ves la tele? ¿Qué clase de programa te gusta más? ¿Cuál es tu programa favorito? ¿Qué día lo dan? ¿A qué hora? ¿Cuánto dura? ¿Por qué te gusta? ¿Cómo es el actor/la actriz principal?*

Guía de televisión

Poll/Survey Form

Objective

To provide opportunities to collect and analyze data and report results in Spanish.

Procedure

Duplicate and distribute the forms for students to fill out and use. You may prefer to fill out the top and left side of the form before duplicating.

Applications

- Students make a list of their favorite activities, foods, movies, clothes, places, and so forth. Then take a class poll by asking students to raise their hands when you read a list of activities, foods, and so on. Either use the form on an overhead projector or copy it on the chalkboard. Write the list of activities or whatever category you choose along the top of the form. Indicate the number of students who choose that activity by placing tally marks in the appropriate box. Students like to see whose preferences most closely resemble those of the class as a whole.

- Along the top of the form, students write infinitives of popular activities, foods, or items in whatever category is decided. They then go around the room and interview each other. They write the name of the students interviewed on the left and check off the positive responses to questions such as *¿Te gusta patinar? ¿Te gustan los huevos?* When the interviews are completed, students report to the class: *A María le/A cinco estudiantes les gusta patinar.*

- Students interview classmates about how often they do certain activities. Along the top of the form, students write *Nunca, A veces, A menudo, Siempre.* Along the left column, they write a certain number of activities. After asking a set number of classmates *¿Cuándo haces ejercicio? ¿Cuándo vas a pasear?* and so forth, they indicate the answers by placing tally marks in the appropriate boxes. Extend the activity by having students report on the results: *Tres estudiantes hacen ejercicio a menudo.*

- Students can use the grid on page 44 to graph the results of their polling.

Concrete Poetry

Objective
To provide structured opportunities for writing simple poetry in Spanish.

Procedure
Discuss the concept of concrete poetry, that is, poetry written in a particular shape. The poem can be written inside the shape or around the edges. The form and appearance of the poem are representations of the poem itself, which is why it is described as concrete. Duplicate and distribute either the diamond or the tree shape, and brainstorm ideas. (You may want to use the grid paper on page 44 for designing additional shapes for concrete poems, or let students do that.)

Applications
- Have pairs write poems using the diamond shape following this format: On the first line, write a noun. On the second line, write two adjectives describing the noun. On the third line, three verbs that tell what the noun does. On the fourth line, two more adjectives. On the fifth line, repeat the noun.

- The **cinquain** is a related form. Have students write cinquains on a topic that you or they suggest. They can follow this format: Follow the first three steps for the diamond poem above. On the fourth line, write a brief sentence about the noun. On the fifth line, write a synonym of the noun or some other related word.

- Have students suggest other shapes for their poems. Poetry writing can be an individual or group activity. Display completed poems in the classroom.

- Let students experiment with the **haiku** format. This Japanese poetry form has three lines totalling seventeen syllables. The first and third lines have five syllables each; the second has seven. Writing haiku is an enjoyable and practical way to teach, review, and strengthen the concepts of syllabification and stress.

- Students may also enjoy writing **acrostics,** in which each line begins with a letter of the key word. For example, an acrostic poem based on the name Juana might look like this:

Joven
Única
Amable
Nada
Atrevida

58

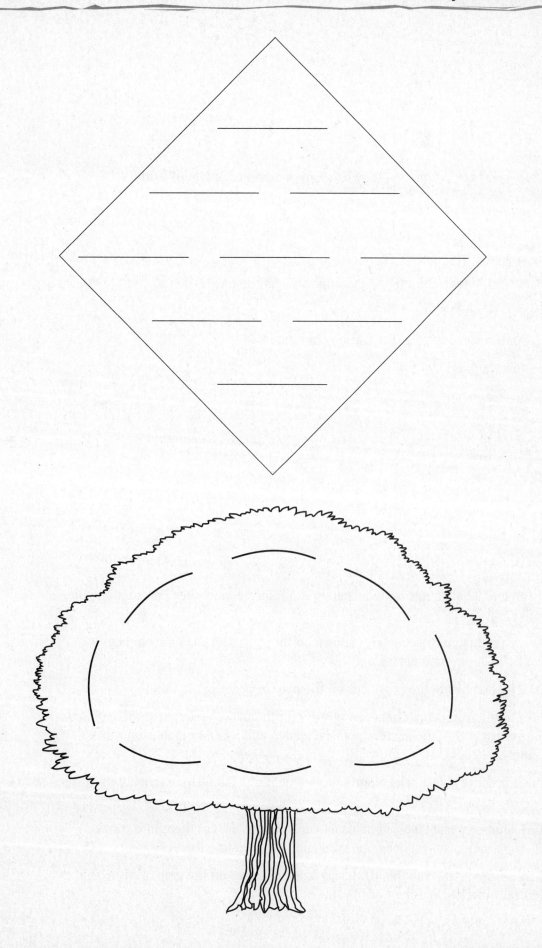

Maps

Objective
To develop map skills, reinforce knowledge of geography, and gain cultural insights.

Procedure
Choose one of the following maps, and duplicate and distribute it.

South America (page 62)

Mexico, Central America, and the Caribbean (page 63)

Central America (page 64)

Mexico City (page 65)

Spain (page 66)

United States (page 67)

California (page 68)

Texas (page 69)

Applications
- Have pairs label countries and capitals and indicate any other information you would like.

- Have pairs match the countries shown on the map with the national flag (pages 75-76) and monetary unit (page 70).

- Have pairs indicate the provinces on the map of Spain.

- Have small groups match the countries with the name and date of the national holiday (page 11), the current political leader, and a fact or facts about the country.

- Have students give a brief biographical sketch of a famous personality from the country.

- Have students paste labeled maps on cardboard, then cut them into puzzle pieces. Groups can exchange puzzles and put them together.

- Have students indicate the Maya and Aztec empires on the map of Mexico, Central America, and the Caribbean.

- While students look at their labeled maps, give descriptions in Spanish of a country including such information as the capital, chief cities, location, names of bodies of water, and so forth. Students identify the country from your description. You can turn this activity into a writing assignment by having groups write brief descriptions and exchange them.

- Assign a country to pairs of students. Have them do research and make product maps. Have two pairs make Venn diagrams of their assigned areas showing similarities and differences in natural resources, geography, industry, and so forth.

- On the U.S. map, have students color and label states, cities, and towns that have Spanish names. Then hold a discussion about the origin and meaning of the names.

- On the map of the U. S., have students mark and label the routes of the Spanish explorers and/or those parts of the country that once belonged to Spain or Mexico.

- On the map of California, have students trace the *Camino Real*, locating and labeling the Spanish missions.

- Assign groups a U.S. state to research. They should find out the names and routes of Spanish explorers, major Hispanic population groups, chief cities, products, and so forth. Invite a social studies class for the group presentations in English. This is a good opportunity for your Spanish students to serve as a resource group.

- Have students look at the maps of South America; Mexico, Central America, and the Caribbean; and Spain, and answer these questions.

    1. Which three continents have Spanish-speaking countries?

    2. What large country in South America is not Spanish-speaking?

    3. If you could choose, which three Spanish-speaking countries would you visit? Why?

    4. Look at the map of Spain. What is the capital? List the names of any Spanish cities you have already heard of.

    5. You are in Surinam and are going to tour the Spanish-speaking nations of South America. If you head from north to south, in what order would you probably visit them?

    6. You are going to visit two Central American countries. Which will you choose? Which will you omit? Give the reasons.

    7. You are in Florida. What Spanish-speaking islands are nearby?

    8. You are in Spain and want to go to the coast. What bodies of water can you choose from?

América del Sur

Límites
Ríos
★ Capitales
● Otras ciudades
⌃ Montañas

Millas
0 100 200 300 400 500 600 700 800

Kilómetros
0 200 400 600 800 1,000 1,200

México, América Central y el Caribe

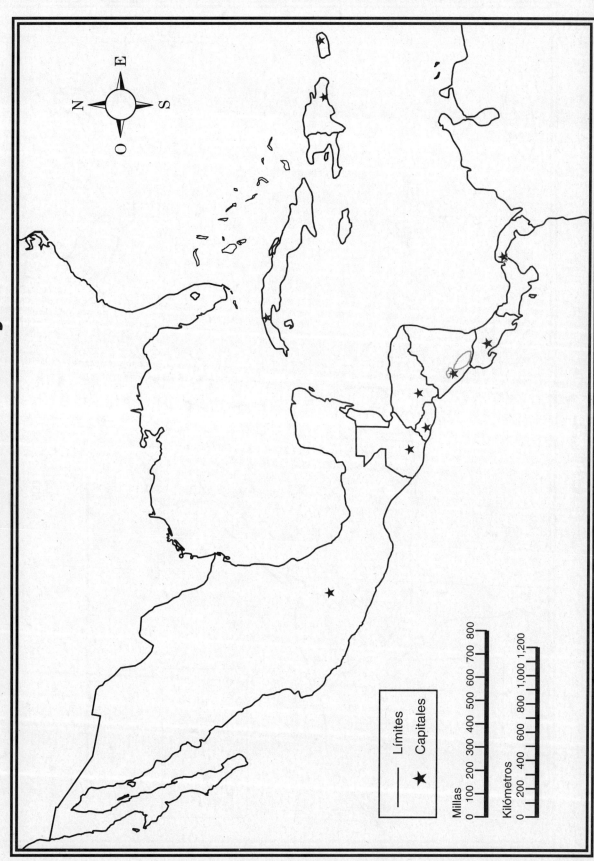

Límites

★ Capitales

Millas
0 100 200 300 400 500 600 700 800

Kilómetros
0 200 400 600 800 1,000 1,200

América Central

N
E
O
S

Límites
★ Capitales
∧ Montañas

Millas
0   100   200   300   400   500

Kilómetros
0   200   400   600   800

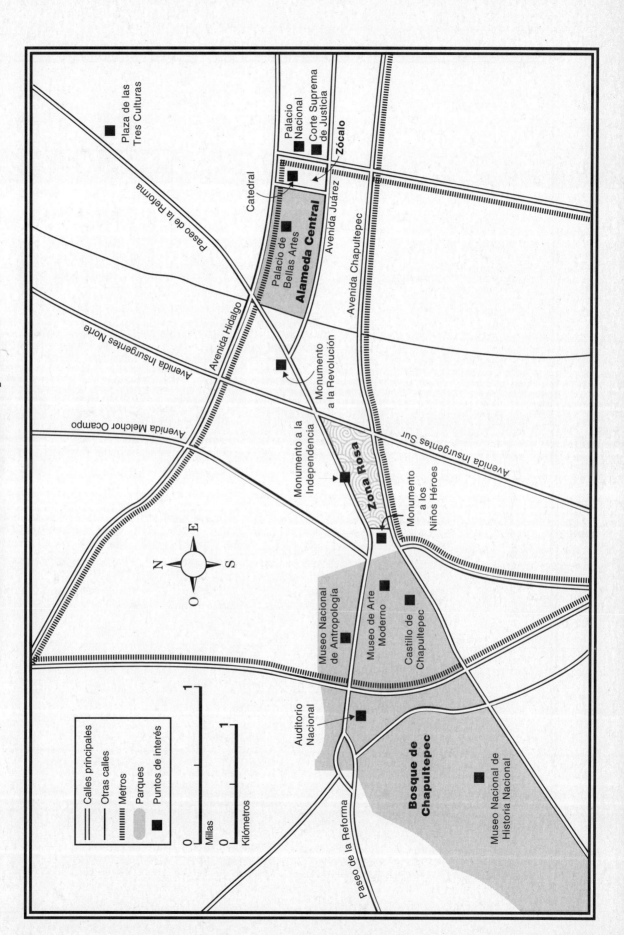

Centro de México, D.F.

Plaza de las Tres Culturas

Palacio Nacional

Corte Suprema de Justicia

Zócalo

Paseo de la Reforma

Catedral

Palacio de Bellas Artes

Alameda Central

Avenida Juárez

Avenida Chapultepec

Avenida Hidalgo

Avenida Insurgentes Norte

Monumento a la Revolución

Avenida Melchor Ocampo

Monumento a la Independencia

Zona Rosa

Avenida Insurgentes Sur

Monumento a los Niños Héroes

N E S O

Museo Nacional de Antropología

Museo de Arte Moderno

Castillo de Chapultepec

Auditorio Nacional

Bosque de Chapultepec

Paseo de la Reforma

Museo Nacional de Historia Nacional

Calles principales

Otras calles

Metros

Parques

Puntos de interés

Millas

Kilómetros

0   1

0   1

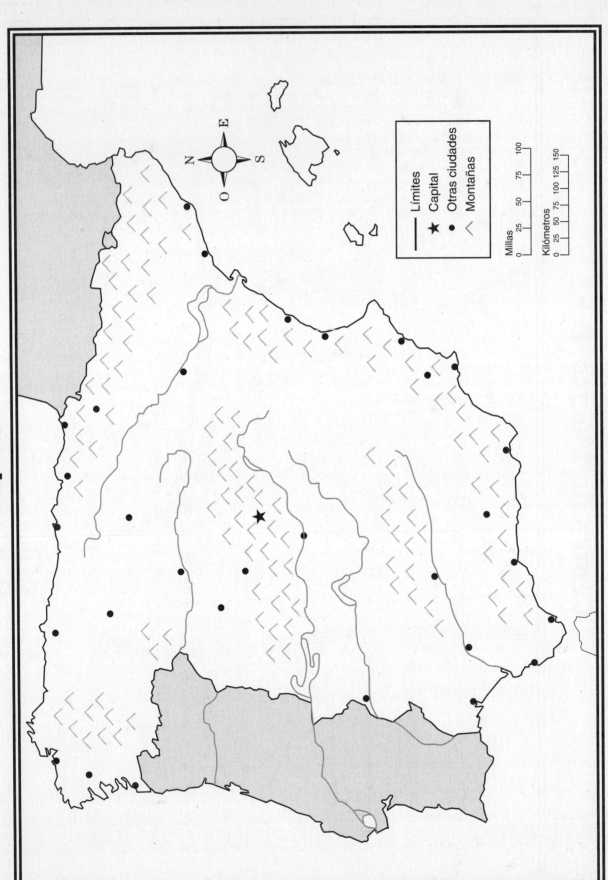

España

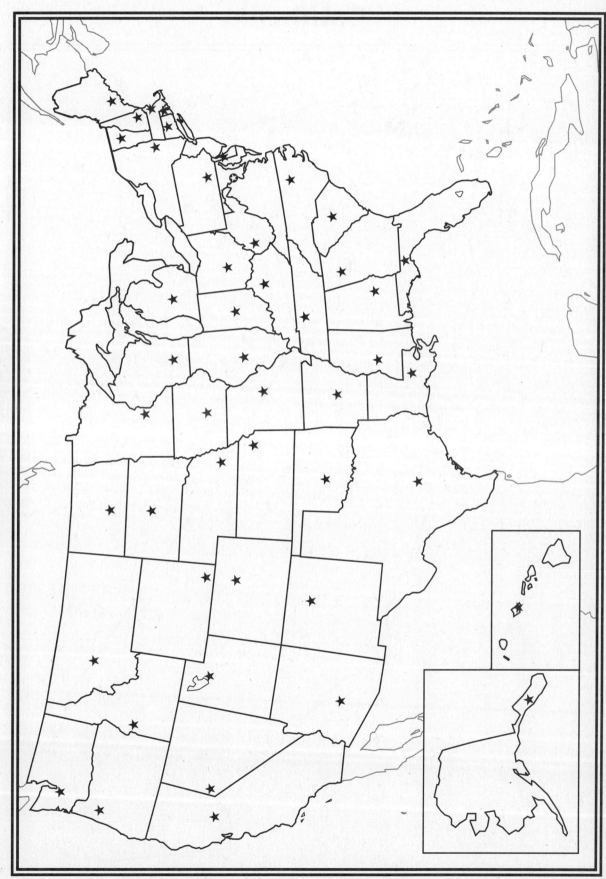

Estados Unidos

California

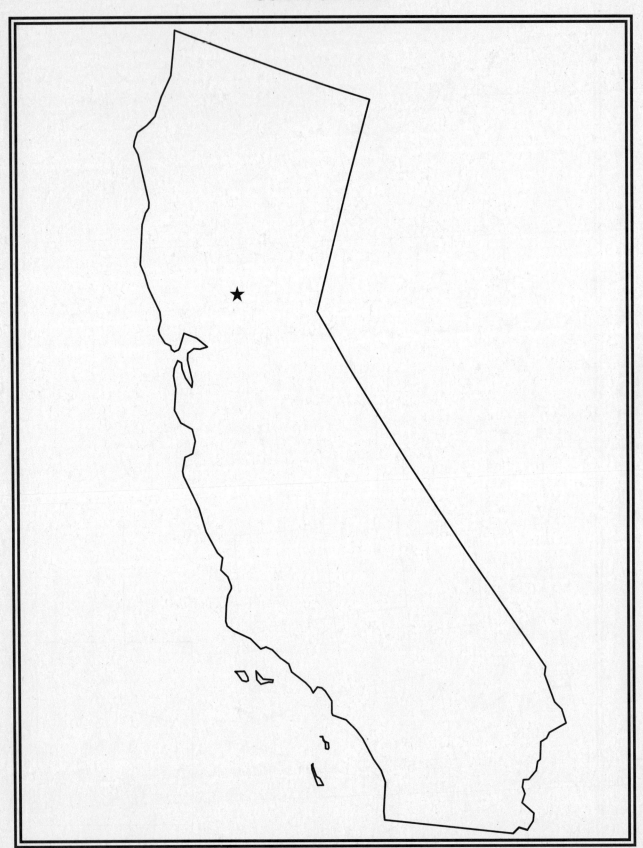

Texas

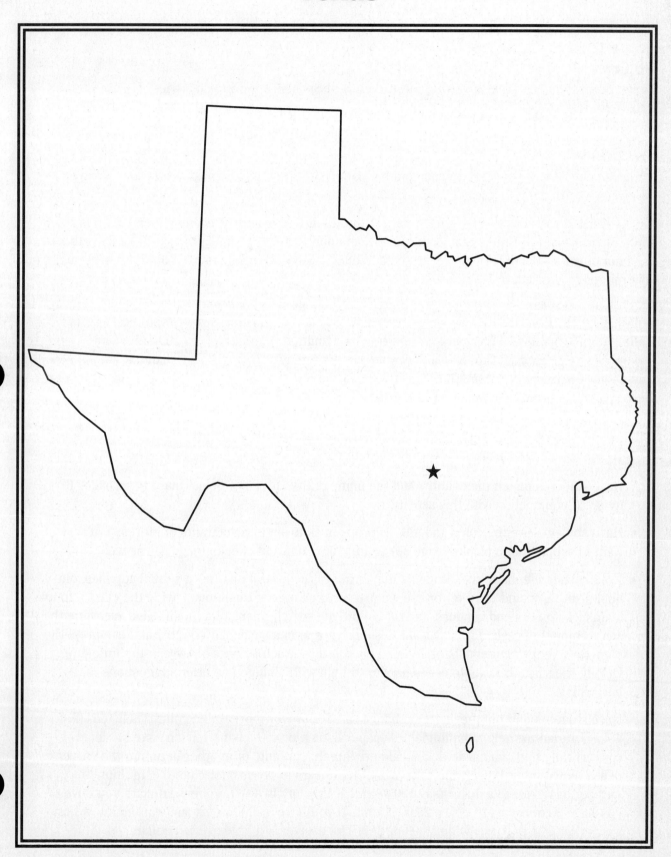

Coins and Bills

Objective
To use Spanish in role-plays involving the currency of Spanish-speaking countries.

Procedure
Duplicate and distribute sheets of coin and bill patterns. Have students paste them to oak tag or lightweight cardboard for greater durability.

Here is a list of the Spanish-speaking countries and their currencies. (Because Puerto Rico is a commonwealth of the United States, the American dollar is the national currency.) The $ symbol is used not only for U.S. dollars but for all the currencies listed here. It was used on the first Spanish coin minted in Mexico.

Argentina . . . . . *peso*	Ecuador . . . . . *sucre*	México . . . . *peso*	Puerto Rico. . . *dólar*
Bolivia. . . . . *peso*	El Salvador . . . *colón*	Nicaragua . . *córdoba*	República
Chile . . . . *peso*	España. . . . . . *peseta*	Panamá . . . . *balboa*	Dominicana . . *peso*
Colombia . . . . . *peso*	Guatemala . . *quetzal*	Paraguay . . *guaraní*	Uruguay . . . . . . *peso*
Costa Rica. . . . *colón*	Honduras . . *lempira*	Perú . . . . *sol*	Venezuela. . . *bolívar*
Cuba . . . . *peso*			

Applications
- Have students match the country and the name of the currency. Select maps from pages 62–64 to use in conjunction with this activity.

- Have students use the coins and bills as props in skits set in restaurants or stores. You may want to supply menu blanks (page 39) and blank restaurant checks (page 41) as well.

- Hold a white elephant sale. Students may bring in recycled items (used school supplies, old books and toys, and the like) or use pictures or drawings of the items. Divide the class into two teams, customers and vendors, and have students switch roles at midpoint. Give everyone the same amount of cash. You may want to set the scene in a particular country and use properly named currency. Students bargain to buy and sell as much as possible within the time limit. During the sale, circulate to act as banker to help with change and offer suggestions for bargaining.

- Have students find out the latest exchange rate for one or more of the countries listed. (Ask your librarian for help in finding a newspaper listing, or call a bank.) Then have students convert the price of a movie ticket, cafeteria lunch, clothing, or another item into the currency of a given country. If you want to convert U.S. dollars to *pesetas,* for example, multiply the number of *pesetas* to a dollar (say 120 *pesetas* = 1 dollar) by the number of dollars you have. If you have 20 dollars: 120 x 20 = 2,400 *pesetas*. If you have 5,000 *pesetas* and want to know how much that is in dollars, divide 5,000 by 120. The answer is a little over 40 dollars.

International Road Signs

Objective
To provide meaningful opportunities to give instructions or directions in Spanish.

Procedure
Duplicate and distribute the sheet of signs. You may want to discuss the meanings of the road sign symbols in English before having students brainstorm their Spanish equivalents. If necessary, write the Spanish words on the chalkboard. Students don't need to produce an exact Spanish equivalent but should convey appropriate meaning.

Applications
- Give one sheet of signs to each student. He or she writes the meaning of the symbols in the blanks. In groups, have students compare sheets and select the most appropriate descriptions.

- Separate and enlarge the signs and paste each one onto a large index card. Write a list of the symbol meanings in random order. Divide the class into two teams. Give team A the index cards and team B the list. Students on team A take turns holding up an index card and asking *¿Qué es esto?* Students on team B take turns answering from the list. Keep score of team B's performance and reverse the procedure.

- For a variation of the previous activity, have students on team B take turns saying *Muéstrame (una bicicleta)*. Students on team A have to hold up the correct sign and say *Aquí está*.

- Use the road signs in conjunction with game board activities (page 24). Paste symbols in game board boxes and have players identify them before proceeding.

- Additional signs (hotel, phone, post office, hospital, restaurant, and gas station) appear on page 42 of the *Writing, Audio & Video Activities* that accompany *Paso a Paso B*. Duplicate and use them to give directions or to practice prepositions of location.

Flags

Objective
To acquaint students with the flags of Spanish-speaking countries.

Procedure
Duplicate and distribute the two pages of flags. Flags identified by country appear in color on the back cover of this book.

Applications
- Have students color and label the flags. Refer them to the back cover for a self-check.

- Describe 10 flags and have individuals or groups identify them orally. A similar activity can be a homework assignment. Prepare simple written descriptions of the flags: *Es roja, azul y amarilla. Tiene un escudo en el centro*. Give the descriptions to students to identify *(Es la bandera de Ecuador)*. This activity provides a good review of colors and vocabulary.

- Individuals or groups can choose a flag and research the meaning of its design and colors. Then they can design their own flag using designs and colors as meaningful symbols. Students can make T-shirts with their flag designs.

- Students each choose a flag and ask partners or group members questions about the country their flag represents: *¿Cuál es tu país? ¿Dónde está? ¿Cuál es la capital?*

- Hold a contest to see which student, pair, or group can name the most flags. You might have the winners of one class compete against winners in another class. Other students should be listening and watching so that it will be a learning experience for them.

- Paste flags in the boxes of the game board (page 25). Students must correctly identify the countries before moving the number of spaces shown on the number cube (page 27).

- Paste flags on individual index cards, and place them in a pile face down. Students in turn choose a card and identify the country before moving the number of spaces shown on the number cube.

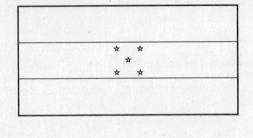

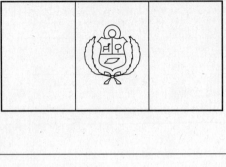

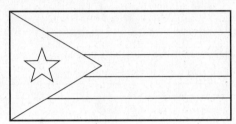

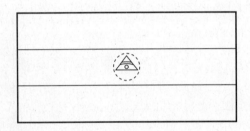

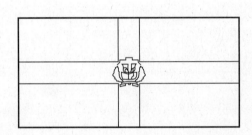

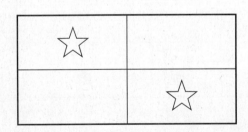

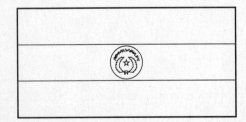

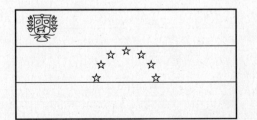

Pronoun Icons

Objectives

To use visuals to reinforce students' understanding of subject and object pronouns and possessive adjectives and their use.

Procedure

Duplicate and distribute the two sheets of icons.

Applications

- As you call out each pronoun or possessive adjective *(nosotros, nuestro, nos)*, have students write it under the correct icon. When individuals have written in all the items, have groups of four fill in one sheet for the group. You may want to call out proper nouns or proper noun + pronoun *(Ana y yo)* as well.

- Divide the class into two teams or into groups of four. Give each team the two sheets to cut up and separate by icon. Call out a noun *(los perros)*, proper noun *(Gloria)*, or possessive adjective *(su)*, and have students hold up and name the correct icon *(ellos, ella; él, ella,* or *usted)*. The first student to hold up the correct icon and say the correct subject pronoun or possessive adjective gains a point for his or her team. To ensure participation by all members, especially students needing extra help, allow team members to consult with one another before answering.

- Play in teams or groups as above. Call out a conjugated verb form *(envían, enviamos)*, and have students show and name all the appropriate subject pronoun icons *(ellos, ellas, ustedes; nosotros, nosotras)*.

- Give groups the two sheets of icons to cut up, separate, and lay face down in a pile. Give groups a set of index cards on which have been written the possessive adjectives. Have students arrange the index cards face up. To win a point, each player must pick an icon from the pile and select the correct possessive adjective card. Players should replace the cards for the next turn.

- Give each group the two sheets of icons to cut up and separate and 15 to 20 index cards on which you (or the students) have written infinitives. The first player picks an icon *(él)* and an infinitive card *(pasear en bote)* and must give the correct verb form *(pasea en bote)*. If he or she does not give the correct form, another group member may do so. Play continues until all group members have had several turns.

- Give groups the two sheets of icons, a game board (page 25), and a number cube (page 27). Have students cut up and separate the icons and place them face down in a pile. Students roll the number cube and pick an icon. In order to move the number of spaces shown on the cube, they must correctly identify the icon by the subject or object pronoun or possessive adjective (whichever is being reviewed) that it represents.

_____ _____

_____ _____ _____ _____

_____ _____ _____ _____

_____ _____ _____ _____

_____ _____ _____ _____

Speech Balloons

Objective

To provide visual support for creating cartoon dialogues in Spanish.

Procedure

Duplicate the sheet of speech balloons. Cut out and enlarge or reduce the balloons as needed, duplicate, and distribute.

Applications

- Have pairs or groups create a comic strip. Have students think of an amusing situation and decide on the characters. They may draw their own or use the cartoon characters on pages 83-85. Students write their characters' speeches in speech balloons and attach them to cartoon frames. Use sheets of blank 8 1/2" x 11" paper as individual frames. Fold sheets in half lengthwise or in quarters, as desired. Display the strips in the classroom, halls, cafeteria, or school offices.

- Collect finished cartoons to create a comic book to share with other Spanish classes.

- Create a cartoon with blank balloons and distribute copies to pairs or groups. Describe a situation, and have students fill in the balloons appropriately. Ask volunteers to share their cartoons with the class. You may want to take a vote for the funniest one.

- Give students a theme and suggest a number of scenes. Brainstorm possible conversations, and then have pairs or groups create a cartoon as above.

- Have students bring in favorite cartoons or comic strips. Paste blank speech balloons over the existing ones, then duplicate and hand out the cartoons. Students write in their own dialogue.

Cartoon Characters

Objective
To provide a visual context for written and spoken activities in Spanish using cartoon characters.

Procedure
Duplicate the sheets of cartoon characters. Cut out specific characters, reduce or enlarge them as needed, and duplicate and distribute. You may want to use these cartoon characters in conjunction with the speech balloons on page 81.

Applications
- Students can use the cartoon characters for cartoon strips, story illustrations, or family trees. You may want to offer them as options for students who are reluctant to draw or provide their own pictures, especially of family members.

- Have students choose one character and write a short biography, including the character's name, age, likes, dislikes, and so forth. Display the biographies on one bulletin board and the cartoon characters on another, and have students match each description with a character.

- Have students choose one cartoon and draw that character's ideal home. A duck, for example, might like to live in a house with a large swimming pool. Students attach the character to a house plan (you may want to duplicate and distribute the graph paper on page 44 for purposes of creating house plans). Have students label the rooms and furniture in Spanish and write a sentence describing what the character does in each room.

- Have students color the clothing on several of the characters and then present them in a group fashion show.

- Have pairs make up a story based on some of the characters, paste the characters on a sheet of paper, and write the dialogue in speech balloons. Ask volunteers to present their cartoons to the class.

Moorish Tiles

Objective

To make a traditional Moorish design and acquaint students with the Arab influence in Spain.

Procedure

Duplicate and distribute the sheet of Moorish tile designs. You may prefer to duplicate the page, cut out only one of the designs, and duplicate and distribute it.

Here is some background cultural information on the Arab influence in Spain that you may want to share with your class.

In 711 an army of Arabs and Berbers, known as the Moors *(los moros)*, crossed the Strait of Gibraltar from Africa and invaded Spain, most of which they dominated from the eighth to the twelfth centuries. The country saw unprecedented achievements in literature, philosophy, mathematics, science, and the arts during this period. The Moorish influence can still be seen in the architecture of such Spanish cities as Granada, with its patios, domes, archways, tiled floors, wrought-iron grillwork, whitewashed walls, and courtyards with central fountains.

Because the religion of Islam prohibits artistic rendering of living things, Arabic art is abstract, not pictorial. The designs are chiefly geometric shapes. The rhythmic, repetitive patterns are most commonly seen today on ceramic tiles used to decorate fireplaces, furniture, and flower boxes, in addition to floors and walls. Muslim blue, a deep, rich color, is a popular choice in the tiles.

Arabic tile designs and architectural features, such as open courtyards, fountains, and iron grillwork, are also common in the southwest United States.

Applications

- Have students color one or more of the patterns with colored pencils or fine-tipped markers.

- Have students make their own Moorish tile design on grid paper (page 44). Display the designs on the bulletin board or in the school hallways.

Ojos de Dios

Objective

To make an *ojo de Dios* ornament and acquaint students with its symbolism and origin.

Procedure

Duplicate and distribute the directions for making an *ojo de Dios*. Your students can make them for decorative wall hangings or ornaments. As a gift, *ojos de Dios* symbolize good wishes from one person to another.

Students may use any texture or weight of yarn, twine, or natural fiber to wind around ice cream sticks, dowels, chopsticks, pencils, craft sticks, or twigs. Supervise students as they work on their projects.

Here is some background cultural information that you may want to share with your class.

The *ojo de Dios* is a diamond-shaped weaving. It is a good luck charm that symbolizes the desire for good fortune, good health, and long life. Its colors are significant. A dark outer border represents safety. Green represents the god of fertility and yellow, the sun god. To bring rain, it is made in shades of blue. The four points of the cross shape may represent earth, fire, water, and air. The eye, or center, may represent the beginning of prayer.

The *ojo de Dios* may have originated in Peru about 300 B.C. The people best known for making these today are the Indians of Mexico's Sierra Madre region. The Cora, Huichol, Tarahumara, and Tepehuane cultures all make and use these weavings in their daily lives. The Cora use the *ojos* as charms for a healthy life. The Huichol, whose name means "healer," use them as special symbols of life and health associated with the sun, rain, and food. Fathers dedicate *ojos* to the gods on behalf of their newborn children. A father weaves the central eye at the child's birth and adds one section each year for the following five years until the talisman is complete. The Tarahumara and Tepehuane use *ojos* to ward off evil. *Ojos* attached to long sticks are waved over peoples' heads to warn the evil spirits that the people are watched over by the eye of God.

How to make *ojos de Dios*

Materials

Yarn, scissors, and two sticks of the same size. (Optional: Feathers, beads, or tassels for finishing touches.)

Directions

1. Tie sticks together to form a cross. (Figure 1)

2. Tie the end of the yarn to the center of the cross.

3. Weave the yarn over and around each stick, keeping the yarn pulled tight. (Figure 2) To change color, knot together two ends of different-colored yarn. The knot should fall on the back side. Continue wrapping until the sticks are covered with yarn. Tie a small knot at the back and leave enough yarn to make a loop for hanging.

4. You may want to add feathers, beads, or tassels to the ends of the sticks. Hang your decorative piece for everyone to enjoy.

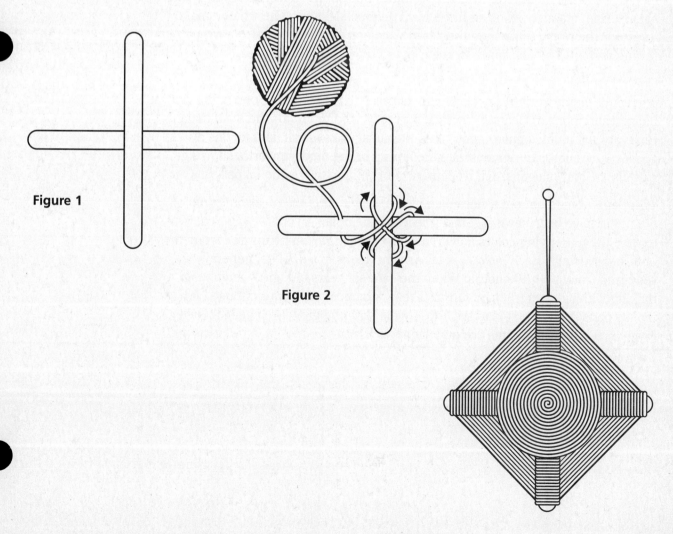

Figure 1

Figure 2

Molas

Objective

To make paper *molas* and acquaint students with their history.

Procedure

Duplicate and distribute the directions for making *molas*. Supervise students as they work on their projects.

Here is some background cultural information that you may want to share with your class.

Molas are the bright fabric artwork of the Cuna Indians of the San Blas Islands of northeast Panama. *Mola* making is a relatively new art form developed in this century. It evolved from an ancient tradition of body painting. *Mola* is a Cuna word meaning "blouse," but today it refers to the panels on the blouse. They are brightly colored and imaginative, using hand-sewn reverse appliqué. The women make the *molas* for the front and back of their traditional garb, which includes a wraparound sarong and a gold nose ring. The men wear modern Western attire.

Central America's last unassimilated indigenous group, the Cuna are preserving a portion of their forested land as a national park. This rain forest, one of the richest biological regions in Central America, serves as inspiration for the *mola* makers. Birds are the most popular motif, but butterflies, sharks, fish, and turtles also appear. Current *molas* demonstrate the impact of the modern world, showing rockets, political slogans, and trademarks, in addition to traditional patterns.

The Cuna women cut out a cloth pattern and sew it onto two to seven layers of cloth that have been sewn together. Pieces of the upper layers are then cut away to expose the underlying colors and create a multicolor design. Later the women embroider details. Each *mola* may take many weeks to complete, generally requiring from 40 to 100 hours. When they are six years old, girls begin *mola* making with just two layers of fabric. These "practice" *molas* are not used for blouse panels, but are sold to tourists. By the time the girls are teenagers, they have made many *molas* and are quite adept artisans.

How to make paper *molas*

Materials
2 pencils, rubber bands, construction paper in a variety of colors, paste, and scissors

Directions

1. Trace the pattern provided on a piece of colored construction paper. (Figure 1) You may prefer to trace around a cookie cutter or draw a simple design found in nature. (For example, a leaf, flower, or fir tree).

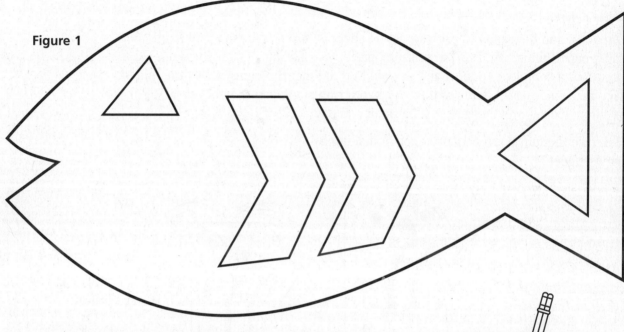

Figure 1

2. Double all the lines by drawing with two pencils fastened together with rubber bands. (Figure 2)

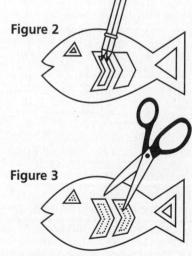

Figure 2

3. Cut out all spaces that do NOT fall between the double lines. (Figure 3)

4. Paste the cutout figure onto construction paper of a contrasting color.

Figure 3

5. Cut around the pasted figure, leaving a border of the second color. (Figure 4)

6. Paste this cutout figure onto another piece of construction paper and cut around it, leaving a border of the new color. Paste the entire piece onto a contrasting background. You can frame your *mola* and display it, or use it as a design for a greeting card.

Figure 4

Hand Puppet

Objective

To stimulate role-playing and skits in Spanish.

Procedure

Duplicate and distribute to each student a sheet of puppet face designs (page 93) and a paper lunch bag. Provide scissors, paste, and markers. Show the students a sketch or a completed puppet and explain that the mouth begins under the folded section. Supervise students as they work, offering suggestions as necessary. For additional ideas, see the cartoon characters on pages 83–85.

Here are the four easy-to-follow steps in making a hand puppet.

 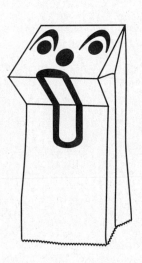  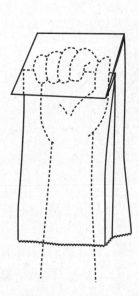

Applications

- Have students use their puppets in skits, role-plays, or monologues. You might suggest situations or characters, or pairs may prefer to supply their own.

- Have pairs make up background information for their puppets, including name, age, address, birthplace, phone number, and so on. Students can then write a short dialogue between the two puppets to perform for the group or class.

- Students may prefer to use their own designs, adding twine or yarn for hair.

- Create a tabletop puppet stage from a large cardboard box. Using a stage adds a professional touch to student performances.

Skeleton Puppet

Objective

To make a traditional skeleton puppet and acquaint students with the celebration of *El Día de los Muertos*.

Procedure

Enlarge, duplicate, and distribute the sheet with the skeleton puppet parts. Help students assemble their puppets, as necessary.

Here is some background cultural information that you may want to share with your class.

The Mexican commemoration of *El Día de los Muertos* is influenced by ancient, pre-Columbian traditions and European Catholic beliefs. November 1 (All Saints' Day) and November 2 (All Souls' Day) are Catholic feast days. The flavor of the Mexican fiesta is a combination and adaptation of both influences, and the celebration is different from any others that honor the dead elsewhere in the world.

Stores are stocked with fiesta supplies many days before the holiday. Stalls sell candy skulls, coffins, and tombstones as well as candles, flowers, incense, special breads, and toys, especially miniature skeletons of paper, wood, cardboard, or papier-mâché. The singing skeleton *(el esqueleto cantante)* is a familiar decorative figure during *El Día de los Muertos* celebrations. Each takes on a different personality, but they all have a big grin. All of these items are used for altars in homes or placed at gravesites.

On November 1, *El Día de los Angelitos*, dead children are honored. A home altar for a child might include a favorite toy, a photograph, and special foods, such as tamales without the spicy chilies. Petals from yellow-gold *cempasúchil*, a kind of wild marigold harvested in late October, are scattered from the front door to the altar, enticing the child's spirit to find the treats on display.

November 2 honors dead adults, so the altar offerings may include strong-flavored foods and photographs of deceased family members. Some families visit the cemetery, clean and restore relatives' graves, and light candles. A holiday bread, *Pan de los Muertos*, is baked in the shape of bones for everyone to share. Friends exchange sugar skulls called *calaveras* with their names written on the forehead.

At first these customs may seem strange to North Americans who are used to more serious commemorations. But seen in the context of a family tradition and a belief in an afterlife, these ways are meaningful.

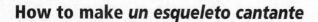

How to make *un esqueleto cantante*

Materials

Oak tag or lightweight cardboard, five brads or paper fasteners, paste, stapler, scissors, and colored markers or crayons.

Directions

1. Paste skeleton parts on oak tag or lightweight cardboard. Cut out all the parts.

2. Carefully poke holes in the body, right arm, and leg parts with a pen or pencil. Attach the leg parts together with two brads, then attach the legs and right arm to the body with the three brads at the designated places.

3. Position and paste or staple the guitar to the left arm and shoulder.

4. Decorate the skeleton with bright colors.

5. Hang in a prominent place to enjoy for *El Día de los Muertos*.

To make a string puppet or simple marionette, tape a dowel rod or pencil to the back of the skeleton. Tie three 12" pieces of string to the back of the three brads that attach the legs and right arm. Tie the pieces of string together. Hold the puppet by the dowel. Pull the string to make the puppet dance.

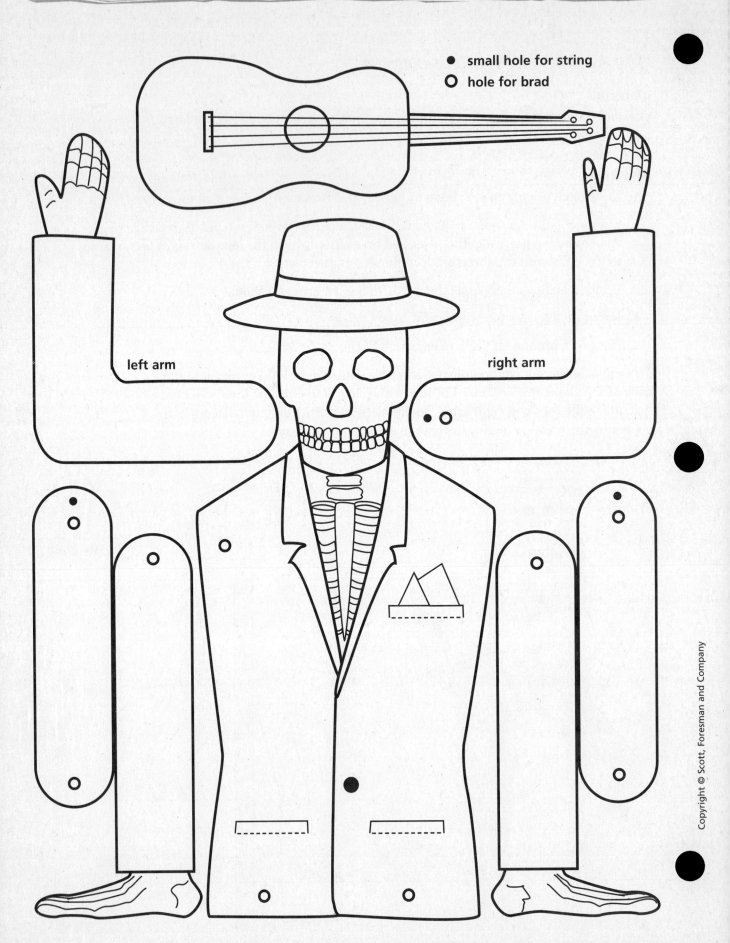

small hole for string

hole for brad

left arm

right arm

Paper Cutouts and Flowers

Objective

To make paper cutouts *(papel picado)* and paper flowers *(flores de papel)* and acquaint students with the *Cinco de mayo* celebration.

Procedure

Duplicate and distribute the directions for making *papel picado* or *flores de papel*. Supervise students as they work on their projects.

Here is some background cultural information on the *Cinco de mayo* celebration that you may want to share with your class.

Cinco de mayo is a celebration of Mexican courage, spirit, and heroism. It commemorates the defeat of invading French troops in the Battle of Puebla on May 5, 1862. After the war for independence from Spain, Mexico owed 80 million *pesos* to other nations. When Benito Juárez, president of Mexico, announced a two-year suspension of foreign payments, France used this default as an excuse to try to annex Mexico.

On May 5, 1862, French general Laurencez was marching toward the capital with 6,000 well-equipped troops when he was met by 4,000 Mexican soldiers in Puebla, 65 miles southeast of Mexico City. Although the Mexicans fought with old muskets, farm tools, machetes, and even stones, one thousand French soldiers lay dead after the first attack.

The French captured the capital in June, 1863, and occupied the country for four years. Nonetheless, the heroic resistance of Puebla is still celebrated not only in Mexico but also widely in the Southwest and other parts of the United States where large numbers of people of Mexican heritage live.

Papel picado, perforated paper cutouts, make colorful, inexpensive banners that you can use as decorations for your *Cinco de mayo* fiesta. Students can also make long garlands of their finished *flores de papel.*

How to make *papel picado*

Materials

Colored tissue paper cut into 12" x 18" sheets, scissors, stapler, and string for hanging.

Directions

1. Spread the tissue paper flat. Fold down 1" on the 18" side for the hanging flap.

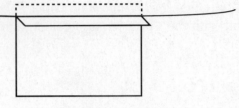

2. Fold the paper in half on the 12" side and crease on the fold to make a sharp line.

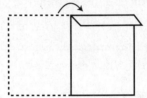

3. Fold the paper diagonally twice.

 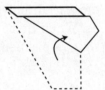

4. Cut out designs along the folded edge. Experiment with snowflake designs.

5. Cut a scalloped design on the outside edge.

6. Open the cutout flat and staple to a string to hang across a room to decorate for a fiesta.

   For a *Cinco de mayo* celebration, you may want to use white, red, and green tissue paper to represent the Mexican flag.

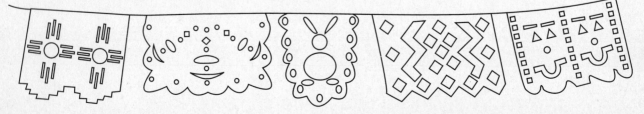

How to make *flores de papel*

Materials
Colored tissue paper cut into 5" or 6" squares, twist ties or short pipe cleaners, scissors.

Directions
1. Stack six to eight sheets of tissue paper together flat and even.

2. Fan-fold the whole stack in 1/2" folds. (Figure 1)

3. Tighten the twist tie in the center of the folded sheets. (Figure 2)

4. Carefully pull open one sheet at a time from each side. Pull first from the right side and then from the left until all of the "petals" are open. (Figure 3)

You can change the size of the tissue paper to make bigger or smaller flowers. You can also use several colors of tissue paper in one flower. In step 3, you can round off the ends of the folded sheets for a rounded petal effect.

Figure 1

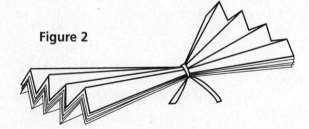

Figure 2

Figure 3

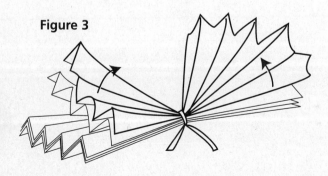

Luminarias

Objective

To make *luminarias* and acquaint students with their symbolism and history.

Procedure

Duplicate and distribute the directions for making *luminarias*. Supervise students as they work on their projects.

Here is some background cultural information that you may want to share with your class.

To celebrate the Christmas season in Mexico and the southwest United States, countless paper bags, tons of sand, and candles are transformed into flickering outdoor lanterns called *luminarias*. They are lined up along window ledges, walkways, and roofs and lit to welcome visitors.

This tradition dates back more than 300 years, when Spanish villagers along the Rio Grande in the United States built bonfires to light and warm their way to church on Christmas Eve. The *luminarias* used today go back to the 1820s, when traders introduced brown wrapping paper into the region. The logs used in the bonfires were replaced by candles set in sand in the bottom of paper bags.

Applications

- Take pictures of the students' completed *luminarias* for a bulletin board display.

How to make *luminarias*

Materials
12" paper lunch bags, sand, small flashlights, and scissors.

Directions
1. Trace a pattern on one side of the bag, leaving at least 4 inches at the top and 3 inches at the bottom. You may want to use this pattern or create your own.

2. Cut out the design, cutting through both sides of the bag. (Figure 1)

3. Open the bag and fold down a 2" cuff around the top. (Figure 2)

4. Fill the bag 1/4 full of sand.

5. Place a small flashlight in the sand in the bag. (Figure 3)

6. Place the completed *luminarias* along your walkway, turn on the small flashlights, and enjoy these symbols of hope and joy for any special occasion.

Variations
1. Use white or brightly colored bags.

2. Paste white or pastel tissue paper behind the cut-out design.

3. Cut a scalloped edge along the top of the bag instead of folding down a cuff.

4. Instead of sand, use soil, kitty litter, or gravel to hold the flashlight in place.

Figure 1

Figure 2

Figure 3

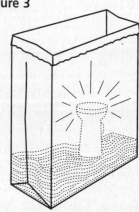

Grids for Interdisciplinary Activities

Objective

To use grids as tools for developing, organizing, and sharing information.

Applications

Conexiones grid

This grid is set up for use with two activities. Have students identify the *Conexiones* activity in *Paso a paso* by writing the guiding question(s), textbook chapter, and page number on the top two lines and the names of those working on the activity at the bottom. In one of the boxes have students write the name of the subject or discipline involved and answers to the question(s). Using the *Mapa de productos* on page 164 of *Paso a paso A* as an example, these answers would include the names of the products shown on the map of Central America that grow in your area, the names of those products that grow in another part of the United States, the student's conclusions about similarities in regions, and the explanation of where bananas are grown. This grid might be an appropriate item to include in the student's portfolio.

You and/or students may want to share the completed grid with the teacher of the appropriate discipline and encourage his or her input.

Interdisciplinary Planning Chart *(for teacher use)*

This is a valuable tool for organizing interdisciplinary units and activities. It graphically presents information on themes and topics that you will focus on during the year. Write the name of your textbook(s) at the bottom. In each box write the theme for that month, the appropriate text chapter(s), class projects, and major test dates. (If you need more space for greater detail, use the chart for five months instead of ten and adjust the boxes accordingly.) Share your chart with teachers of other disciplines so that you can reinforce each other's curriculum.

You might want to share your chart with your department head or principal, with parents, and even perhaps with the class.

Interdisciplinary Learning Activities Chart *(for teacher use)*

This grid is a useful tool for exploring how a particular theme or topic is covered in different disciplines. Write the name of a different school subject on the line in each box. Write the question for discussion in the box at the top; for example, How are different holidays celebrated in various cultures? For your Spanish class, you might include whole class discussion, making paper cutouts or another craft project associated with a specific holiday in the Spanish-speaking world, individual family research and presentations, making Spanish greeting cards, creating a crossword puzzle using Spanish seasonal vocabulary. You or your colleagues fill in the remaining portions of the grid.

Conexiones

Interdisciplinary Planning Chart

Subject _____

Grade Level _____

Teacher _____

September	October	November	December _____	January _____
February	March	April _____	May _____	June _____

TEXT(S):

104

Interdisciplinary Learning Activities Chart

Spanish

Activities: I = Individual, G = Group, C = Class